The Po

# The Powerboat Handbook

JIM MARTENHOFF

Winchester Press

While some of the photos in this book were taken by the author, the book could not have been illustrated adequately without the assistance of Mercury Marine, Johnson, and Evinrude Motors, who supplied most of the pictures. The author is also indebted to the Boating Industry Association, for supplying much of the technical artwork.


*Library of Congress Catalog Card No.: 74-16872*
*ISBN: 87691-166-1*

*Published by Winchester Press*
*205 East 42nd Street, New York 10017*

*Second printing 1976*

*Printed in the United States of America*

# *CONTENTS*

# FOREWORD

Cruise down any suburban street in America, and you will probably see the prows of small boats protruding from garages, carports, or houses. It's not unusual to count three or four boats to the block, particularly in areas near good waterways.

Boating is a family pastime, rapidly gaining new adherents daily. A half-million craft are added to America's recreational navy every year, and at last count the total was in the neighborhood of eight million assorted boats. They range from the billionaire's posh yacht down to dented aluminum canoes, but the bulk are small powerboats, mostly outboards, and the increasingly ubiquitous "sterndrives," which are a marriage of outboard and inboard.

Powerboating means action, action geared to every member of the family. There's waterskiing, swimming, skindiving, fishing, beachcombing, cruising, exploring, camping by boat, and picnics ashore and afloat—healthful outdoor exercise, coupled with a sense of adventure and the chance to get away from it all.

With the help of a boat you can still find quiet coves, with calm waters ruffled only by the occasional splash of a fish. You can still enjoy blazing dawns and sunsets. There is peace, contentment, with the opportunity for fascinating adventure as counterpoint. Small wonder so many families take the plunge, when someone says, "Dad, let's buy a boat."

Maybe you've already gotten your feet wet in boating, and own a small powerboat. Perhaps you are only contemplating it. Maybe you even feel like an old-timer, and are about to trade up for a larger craft, the inevitable and not necessarily unhappy fate of all boatowners. Whatever class you are in, you can profit from reading this book. It can save you money and sweat; it can make you a safer, happier, and more knowledgeable skipper; and, hopefully, it will do these things with plain talk and common sense—no abstruse studies, no bewildering, technical jargon. So if you're ready to learn how to select, maintain, and operate a powerboat—with maximum ease and enjoyment and minimum worry and expense—then please read on.

Jim Martenhoff
Miami, Florida
March 1, 1975

*PART ONE*

# *Selecting a Powerboat*

# *BEFORE YOU BUY*

Before you invest any money in a powerboat, invest some time in learning all you can about boats and boating. You'll find that the hours you spend educating yourself will pay important dividends when it comes time to make a purchase.

## *Free Boating Classes*

Probably no other sport in history has developed such a framework of helpful volunteer organizations as has boating. The neophyte skipper can attend free classes in boating provided by a number of groups. There is no charge for the instruction. You pay only for your texts and study materials, a modest outlay, and there's profit in it because you keep them as the start of a boating library.

There are two principal organizations that between them educate several hundred thousand beginning boatmen (and women) each year. The first of these, the United States Power Squadrons, is a nonprofit, civilian group that was born in 1914 when sailing was king and the still-new "stinkpotter" was something of a tolerated abomination among genuine yachtsmen.

The USPS has close to ninety thousand members in almost four hundred local squadrons, a few of them in American business and military colonies overseas. Headquarters is (P.O. Box 345) Montvale,

N.J. 07645. Each local unit teaches the basics of boating to novices in a 10-lesson course with classes usually held one night weekly. Boatmen who join the USPS can go on to take advanced courses offered to the membership, and can take their turns as instructors and proctors in the basic classes, passing on their knowledge to neophytes.

The USPS makes a special effort to reach beginners with a toll-free telephone number from which class information may be obtained. Nationally, it is 800-243-6000; in Connecticut only, it is 800-882-6500. Dial the number, ask for Power Squadron class information, give your postal zip code, and the operator will tell you where and when the next class nearest you will get underway. USPS courses, for the most part, are offered only in late winter and early autumn.

The other prestigious group of volunteers is the U.S. Coast Guard Auxiliary, a nonmilitary adjunct of the service. The USCGA teaches a more comprehensive 12-lesson course, and it is often conducted in twice-weekly classes to shorten the total time obligation. Unlike the USPS, the Auxiliary schedules classes on a year-round basis.

Instruction is only part of their assignment. They also assist the regular Coast Guard in safety patrols and towing of disabled boats. They patrol regattas and other organized water programs. A solid service is the Auxiliary's "Courtesy Motorboat Examination." They will inspect your boat and advise you where you may be lacking in safety equipment or installations. You can take care of any inadequacy and, upon a second examination, receive a "CME" decal for your boat. You may, of course, pass the examination the first time. This inspection is a valuable service, for the CME decal is usually honored by Coast Guard boarding teams and other governmental agencies at the state and local levels.

It's a fact of life on today's busy waterways: you may be halted and boarded at any time for a routine safety inspection. If you lack the required gear, it may mean both a citation from a state or other patrolman, answerable in court, and a citation from the Coast Guard, for which no court appearance is called for. You may either pay a fine or write a letter explaining the circumstances, in which case the fine

*A Coast Guard Auxiliarist examines a boat in a safety check.*

may be forgiven. It usually is, if you show you corrected the defect. When boarding officers see the CME decal, they usually sheer off, which spares you lost time afloat.

Your best bet for locating USPS and USCGA classes in your area is to ask the local marine dealer. He may be a member of one or the other; and almost certainly would know if such an organization has a local unit.

Other organizations which may offer classes in your region are the American Red Cross, which has comprehensive water safety programs, and the Coast Guard Reserve, which has been experimenting with several short, speedy courses that serve as an introduction to boating. In some parts of the country the various parks and recreation departments of local governments offer instruction.

No one who is a novice in boating should pass up an opportunity to attend a free boating class. Your investment in time is repaid many times over in a sense of assurance when you first take command of the family's little vessel.

As a bonus, you rub elbows with experts, explore the finer points of boating with instructors during the inevitable coffee breaks, and often make fast friends among fellow students who may skipper their own craft, in company with yours, on future expeditions afloat.

The best way to begin in boating is to attend a class. And if a curious reader is wondering why this book is necessary at all, since so much knowledge can be gained from a blackboard, there is this explanation.

Much of what follows will not be found in conventional teaching texts. It provides a more rounded knowledge, particularly in the areas of operation and maintenance, than you can find in most books or classes.

## *Seek and Ye Shall Learn*

It pays to ask questions. For some odd reason, a man will go out and buy a small powerboat, manage to get it into the water, and head out beyond the nearest horizon, all on the blind assumption he did everything right and will never make a mistake.

The investment you make in a boat is somewhat more money than you fork over for a fly rod, a set of golf clubs, or most other sporting paraphernalia, and it's smart business to protect your equity. If you have never owned a boat, or have owned only smaller, inexpensive skiffs, ask questions.

A good place to start your curiosity act is at a boating class. Seek advice on boats, brand names, dealers, ramps, facilities, and places to go in your boat.

Since we are slowly approaching the subject of boats, pay particular attention to the makes available in your area. Boating has its "brand X" problems, too, and some boats are definitely inferior to others. Delicate snoopery can save you money by at least uncovering the names of some dogs, glossied up in the shape of boats but still apt

*Boat shows are boating "supermarkets."*

to misbehave in public. No one is so willing to talk as the man who feels he got stung.

When you do go shopping for a boat, don't jump at the first deal, no matter how attractive it may appear. Look at several others, and if by comparison that first deal still shines, then go back to it. You aren't buying an appliance when you buy a boat; there's a lot of cash involved. You want to be satisfied. So shop around, compare the features of one boat with another.

If a boat show is scheduled within easy driving distance, by all means attend. Boat shows are marine supermarkets. A broad variety of craft are assembled under one roof, and you can equal a week or more of "comparison shopping" in just an afternoon.

You may even think of asking your local newspaper outdoor columnist for advice. He can probably help you in general terms, though he may be reluctant to suggest particular brand names since his recommendation constitutes a somewhat unethical endorsement.

Snooping around on the edge of nautical circles will give you a good base from which to take a further step. You will at least have some idea of what makes of boats are available in your region, and who the dealers are.

*Visit public launching ramps to get an idea of the most popular brands of boats.*

## *Narrowing Your Choices*

At all costs, avoid the so-called "shade-tree" brands. Unhappily, it is still relatively easy to go into the boatbuilding business, at least so far as fiberglass is concerned. Fiberglass is easily molded. You take any combination of glass cloth, mat—which is a random-fiber sheet—and roving, woven of heavier skeins, wet it down with a thermosetting polyester resin, and it will conform to virtually any shape.

People have "borrowed" existing boats, disassembled them, used fiberglass to make female molds of hull and deck, reassembled and returned the original boat, and gone into business. It is still being done, although the piracy is not as widespread as was formerly the case. Obviously anyone who will "pop" a copy is not to be trusted. His hull may appear equal to the original in appearance, but inadequacies in construction, while not evident to the eye, make it decidedly inferior.

Nationally advertised brands are safer buys. So are those regional brand names which have acquired considerable popularity. Check the advertisements in local and national boating or outdoor publications. Visit popular launching ramps, note the names of boats as their owners launch them. You'll see some names repeated frequently. Talk to boatowners for a moment or two.

The better-known makes of boats offer another bonus, even if they seem a little higher in first cost. They generally have better resale values, bring more money when you trade or sell. Off-beat makes and shade-tree boats have far less value on the second-hand market. In the end, you lose far more than you save by what seems an attractive retail list price.

By shopping around and not being afraid to ask questions, you will eventually wind up with a good idea of the boat you want.

## *Choosing a Dealer*

Your marine dealer may become the best commercial friend you ever made, so pick him with some care. Find out if he goes boating himself, or fishing, or skiing. Most are reasonably active in boating, which is how they probably got in the business in the first place—under the mistaken impression it would be more fun than selling insurance, or whatever they did formerly. Actually, it's a tough and highly competitive trade. The average dealer puts in long hours, and has little spare time. But he should know a good deal about boating and allied water sports.

It's a shame to appear downbeat and negative on newcomers, but the longer a dealer has been in business the better it is for the buyer. He represents stability. By all means wangle an opportunity to view his service facilities, for there's a world of difference between a

*Pick your dealer with care. He can be a big help to you.*

gangling youth with a rusty wrench and a shop full of tools manned by competent mechanics. And a few discreet inquiries may reveal whether the dealer is a man who honors his warranties or a rascal who refuses to recognize a buyer once he has pulled away from the shop with his new boat. Financial institutions are notably discreet about the affairs of customers, but if you know your banker well enough, you might ask him to advise you on the credit rating and prospects of a dealer.

It's a fact: The combination of a shade-tree brand boat and a shabby dealer has ruined the pleasure of many families entering boating. If I dwell upon this subject at tiresome length, it's because of the importance it bears toward really enjoying the sport.

The vast majority of boats *are* worthy, and so are the dealers. Besides, there is more consumer awareness in boating than in possibly any other sport, and Uncle Sam has his arm around your shoulder when you go shopping for a boat.

## *Coast Guard Standards*

Under the authority of the Boat Safety Act of 1971, the U.S. Coast Guard was authorized to develop and promulgate safety standards for boats. They cannot actually tell a builder how to construct a boat. It is assumed he conforms to current and common industry standards in that area.

As an aside, there are such standards and they are in book form. Issuing authorities are two trade groups of impeccable reputation, the National Association of Engine and Boat Manufacturers (NAEBM) and the Boating Industry Association (BIA). The group that lays down the law as far as construction standards are concerned is the American Boat and Yacht Council (ABYC). There is also a marine division of the long-famed Underwriters Laboratory. They test components and equipment, ranging from fuel tanks to fire extinguishers.

Any boatbuilder who adheres to ABYC standards will turn out a good boat. You may even find a BIA Certification Plate on a boat, attesting to the fact that it was built to the standards.

But the Coast Guard also enters the picture. New boats now are

*BIA certification plate means the boat was built to proper standards.*

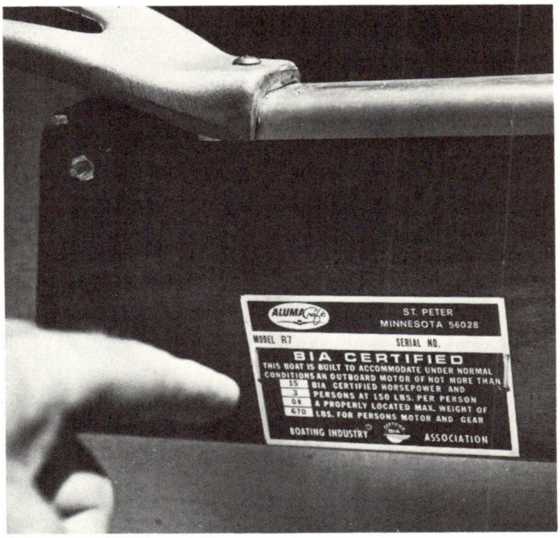

*Coast Guard standards regulate most smaller powerboats.*

required to have a Hull Identification Number, or "HIN." Not only does it help to have this number molded or stamped on the hull, because it aids in case of theft, but it also helps the buyer in case of an unknown defect.

Everyone knows that Detroit auto makers for years have been required to call back cars when latent defects show up after delivery and sale. Such defects are repaired at no cost to the buyer. Well, the Coast Guard enforces a "defect notification program" in the world of boating. Builders have to fix, for free, any problems related to safety that turn up after the boat is built.

Note that the defect must be safety-related. If the upholstery fades as fast as your wife's summer tan, it's strictly a fight between you and the dealer. But if the steering went sour, the Coast Guard is interested. You can notify them of safety-related problems, and they will go to bat for you.

This, however, is why you should avoid the shade-tree brands. Such a builder would—perhaps gratefully—close up shop and seek refuge in the safe harbor of bankruptcy before he'd call back several hundred boats. Better-known builders fix their products for free, and it has happened when minor defects appeared.

All new powerboats under 20 feet long, built after August 1, 1973, must have positive buoyancy in the form of flotation. In other words, it won't sink. You can capsize it, either in a sloppy bit of high-speed maneuvering or by being dumb enough to fare forth in the face of storm warnings, but the boat won't sink. Stay with it until rescued, and you'll have an adventure story to tell but no one will drown.

It's almost impossible to deliberately capsize a properly designed boat, but it can be done if heavily overloaded, with the weight all to one side, and if violently turned at high speed. Hence the flotation rule, which does not apply to canoes, kayaks, or sailboats.

All powerboats under 20 feet long must also have a Coast Guard capacity plate showing the safe-load limit for that particular hull. It is carefully calculated, and fits nearly all conventional hulls.

It's worth digressing to note that the formula doesn't work at all on such older hulls as the famed Banks Dory. This is the boat seen in

*Overloading is dangerous and can capsize a small boat.*

some popular, classic paintings, with slickered fishermen hauling in cod far at sea. According to the formula, it isn't a safe boat when loaded, while the fact is that its form evolved over centuries of experience and, when properly handled, is one of the safest ever devised.

The digression is helpful for anyone who overhears casual waterfront condemnation of the formula. It may not fit the Banks Dory, but then few people buy such boats. And it does work for conventional powerboats, so heed the advice and stay within the load limits.

In the case of outboards under 20 feet, the Coast Guard also requires a plate listing the maximum safe horsepower. Like the load limit, it is advisory. You break no law if you hang a more muscular kicker on the stern. But, as authorities have noted, should you become involved in an accident and your boat is overpowered, you may have an interesting case of civil liability in any litigation that ensues. And the dealer will be in it with you.

In summation, however, you can't go far wrong sticking to a well-known boat, buying it from a reputable dealer, and checking for the standards plates. In the case of an outboard under 20 feet long, far and away the most popular type of boat in America, even Uncle Sam wants you to get a fair deal.

But the rest is still up to you.

# *DESIGN FACTORS TO CONSIDER*

## *Hull Forms and Types*

### *THE BASIC BOAT*

If there is such a thing as the basic boat, it's the box, squared at the ends, with gently curved bottom sections rising at bow and stern, flat on the bottom.

This is the "punt" of an earlier era, and it survives today in slightly more sophisticated form as the "johnboat," popular on quiet, inland waters. It has good load-carrying ability and is easily powered with small outboards. That flat bottom is an efficient skimming dish, so the boat planes handily, rising to run atop the water. It is shallow draft, is easily beached. If the beam is wide enough, it has good lateral stability. It is not "tender," which is the boatman's word for tippy.

However, most johnboats are on the narrow side, are quite tender, and capsize easily if mishandled. They also can be very rough-riding boats in choppy water, and wet, taking a lot of spray aboard. For these reasons their market usually is confined to areas with protected waters.

Next on the scale, and still basic, is the more conventional "skiff," where the blunt, squared-off bow is brought to a point. The bottom may still be flat throughout its length. "Sharpie" is a common name for the type, with an obvious derivation since it has a sharp bow rather than a blunt, square one. It is much like the johnboat or punt in its characteristics.

*Boats come in all shapes and sizes, with wide variety in design.*

*The skiff's hull can make a fine angling platform.*

The sharpie is slightly better in choppy waters, but not much. About all you can say for it is that it produces less spray, although occupants will still get wet when the wind's up. It's largely a dying breed, except at fishing camps where it serves as a rental skiff. Its chief virtue to camp operators is cheap cost and reasonable durability, even if built of plywood.

As a further refinement in design, you have the semi-vee bottom skiff. The bottom forward is faired upward into a vee shape, to provide a sharp entrance at the waterline. It's supposed to knife through the chop, easing the ride. To some extent it does so. However, the bottom is still flat aft. When the boat is up on plane, which means it runs with the bow slightly raised and the flatter bottom sec-

*The skiff has a flat bottom, simple lines, and a vee'd bow.*

*The most basic boat is the boxlike, "punt," or "johnboat."*

tions angled upward, it can beat your brains out in rough going. It thumps from sea to sea, banging and smashing along in a series of shuddering collisions. The only way to beat the problem is to slow down, drop off plane, and ride through the water rather than over it. Progress is slow, and a fishing trip becomes an exercise in boating frustration.

You still see this hull form, and will for years. It has all the other advantages: relatively low construction cost, shoal draft, low power requirements compared to more sophisticated hull forms, good lateral stability and load-carrying capacity. With a proper interior layout designed for fishermen, with built-in conveniences like rod racks and bait wells, it makes a fine angling platform.

*A "deep vee" hull yields a soft ride in bumpy water.*

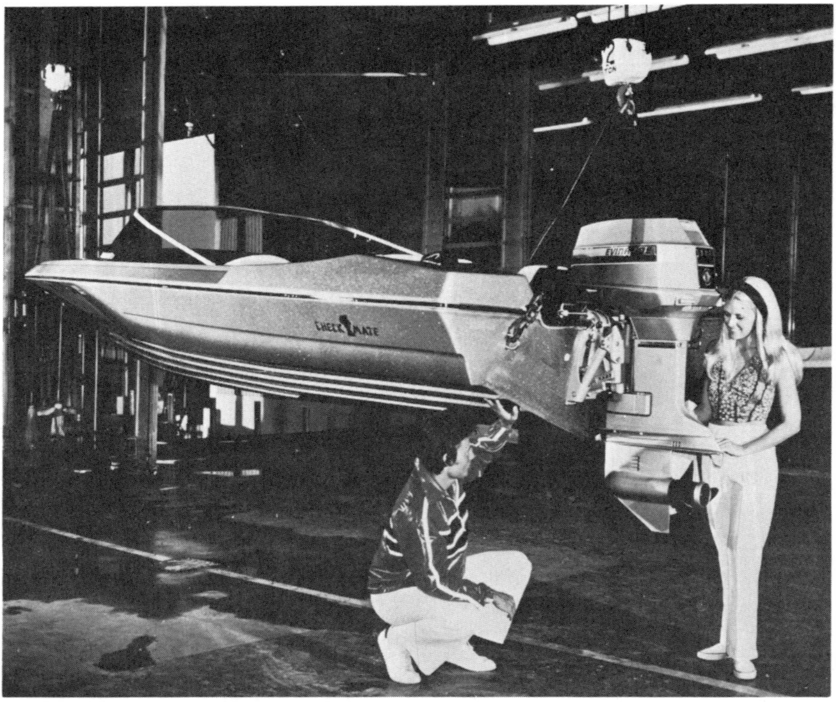

Many modern designs utilizing this hull form beat the rough water problem with a stand-up steering station aft, but it would be overly digressive to explore this factor now. We'll return to it later, deferring to the continuing question of hull forms.

## *THE DEEP VEE HULL*

Obviously, it is the flat bottom sections causing all the performance problems, the rough ride, the pounding. So if you eliminate the flatness, you improve the boat.

Two American designers, independent of each other, came up with the solutions that found favor in the market. Ray Hunt originated the so-called "deep vee." He built a boat with a bottom like a long wedge. It was, in cross section, a deep, sharp, vee-shape.

This eliminated the flat planing surface. To restore it, at least partially, he added "strakes" on each side of the bottom. These are tiny steps, a few inches wide, running the length of the bottom, or nearly so. They offered a little flat surface to the water. When you hit the throttle, the running strakes provided lift, and the hull rose on plane. In a bumpy, rough sea, the wedge-shaped hull just knifed through the water. It simply did not pound, and your teeth remained firmly in place. True, some early models that copied Hunt's lines had problems locating the strakes, and some did prove bumpy, but Hunt's design eventually came to dominate the market for open-water boats.

Hunt originated the design in the late 1950s, and it was proven in the cauldron of offshore powerboat racing. Today, the more sophisticated ocean racing hulls – long, lean, and with knifelike bottoms – can exceed 80 miles per hour in four- and five-foot seas.

## *THE CATHEDRAL AND TRI-HULLS*

At the same time, Hunt was trying to eliminate the flat bottom with a complex bottom configuration. It was not a wedge, like the deep vee. The moldability of fiberglass permitted compound curves you couldn't form with wood or even aluminum. Seen in cross section, the hull was almost "corrugated." It was a series of hulls, side by side.

*Tri-hulls have squared bows, more room aboard.*

This boat hit the market as the famed Boston Whaler, probably the best known name in the world. It was composed of a foam sandwich, with fiberglass outer hulls and polyurethane foam inside. It was unsinkable, even if sawed in half—and they did exactly that as a publicity stunt. It was self-bailing. You could pull the transom drain plug and leave the boat out afloat all night in a downpour of rain. It wouldn't swamp, as so many other small boats did.

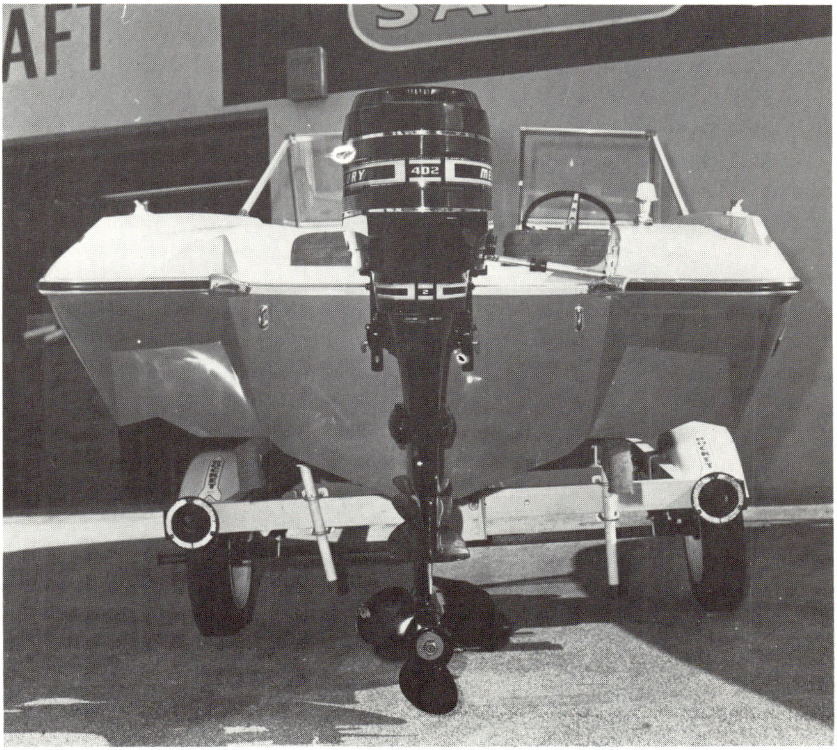


*Stern of tri-hull shows complex bottom configuration.*

And with that complex bottom configuration, it provided a reasonably smooth ride in bumpy water—still a bit rugged, perhaps, but magnificently superior to the skiffs, sharpies, and semi-vees of comparable size.

In this same period, Dick Cole came up with an identical design philosophy. His complex bottom configuration was much like the Whaler's, with enough differences that the two could be patented separately. Cole called his design the "cathedral" hull, meaning the opposite of "dihedral," an aircraft term for wings that are angled upward. Cole had bottom sections toward the chines, or sides, that angled downward. He had a vee cross section in the center, with upside-down vee's alongside—an oversimplification, but valid. Like the Whaler, it took the bump out of boating.

Both designs led to a host of copies. Some were shamelessly molded directly from the original hulls. Some were originated, with variations, by reputable designers intrigued with the essential philosophy. The term "tri-hull" came into being, and soon was applied to nearly all boats of this type, even Cole's—a development that raised his eyebrows somewhat.

Why this second approach when the deep vee was such a proven performer? For several reasons. The deep vee, in smaller lengths, was notoriously tender. You could put your foot on a gunwale (the top, side, edge of a boat) and the whole hull would dip sharply downward. There is a practical lower length limit to deep vees. Most are produced today as larger hulls, say, 20 feet and up. In lengths under 20 feet, the deep vee was compromised in order to maintain lateral stability. The resulting hull was termed a "modified" or "moderate" vee hull.

The cathedral and tri-hulls, on the other hand, had good lateral stability and a comfortable ride in choppy water, although in a really rugged offshore sea they tended to slam at the bow. Because the bows on tri-hulls were blunt and squared off, the boats had more interior space. Small boats had the accommodation capacity of conventional hulls two to four feet longer. They still drew less water than a deep vee, and were more easily beached and operated in shallow areas.

The deep vees and the tri-hulls dominate the entire market today in any major boating area where there is open, potentially bumpy water. But there's one other form of hull that deserves at least brief mention.

## *THE DISPLACEMENT HULL*

In terms of performance, all powerboats fall into two distinct classifications. So far we have been talking about planing hulls.

These are designed with bottom sections that provide lift. Under adequate power, they literally rise above the water to skim atop the surface, a performance characteristic known as "planing."

Speeds can be very high. Racing hydroplanes are planing boats. An unlimited hydroplane set a world record for propeller-driven boats of 200.419 miles per hour. Such speeds are possible only because the hull skims the surface of the water. On racing hydros only the propeller, stabilizing fin, and rudder, are really submerged. The hull itself barely touches the surface of the water.

At the other extreme are the so-called displacement hulls, which sit down in the water, occupying (or displacing) an amount of water equal to their own weight. They aren't meant to plane. They move through the water slowly. The laws of hydrodynamics limit them to a maximum speed roughly equal to 1.5 times the square root of their waterline length. A boat 36 feet long on the waterline can reach a top speed of nine knots (nautical miles per hour). Pour on extra power, and the hull begins to squat at the stern, rolling up such a large bow wave it cannot climb over it. The power and fuel is wasted.

Why bring up displacement hulls at all? Because they seem to be on the verge of a resurgence. They need very little power to move them at their maximum, which is called "hull speed." This is because displacement hulls have long bodies, clean, fine entries, an easy run aft (the hull bottom fairs in toward the stern), relatively narrow beams, and in effect are streamlined in their underwater sections. Bottoms are usually rounded, although not always. Sometimes they are double-ended, or have "canoe" sterns. In fact, your canoe is a perfect example of a hull moved easily with minimum effort.

Obviously an 18-foot displacement hull will be slow. Top cruising speed will be about 6.5 knots, or about 7.5 statute miles per hour, twice a man's easy walking speed.

But in these days of energy problems, displacement hulls seem on the verge of making a comeback. You can propel an 18-footer of clean design with as little as four horsepower, properly geared down to a large, slow-turning wheel (propeller). Fuel consumption hourly, especially with diesel, is so incredibly low that you can cover 10, 12, even 15 or more miles on every gallon of fuel, as opposed to two or three miles on the average planing boat, one mile on larger yachts,

*Trawler yacht is a typical displacement hull.*

and as little as a half mile per gallon on some heavily built semiplaning boats.

There are displacement craft on the market in a variety of sizes and types, down to fishing craft. If you don't have to cruise long distances to the fishing grounds, and have the time, they can be an answer. As an aside, nearly all displacement designs are extraordinarily seakindly, able to take very rough water indeed. When ballasted they are extraordinarily stable and safe craft.

You pays your money and takes your choice, but in areas where they suit the waters and distances, displacement hulls are worthy of consideration.

## *MISCELLANEOUS HULL FORMS*

There are a variety of hull shapes, some historical, that possess limited and usually regional popularity. The Banks Dory, for example, was developed for codfishing on the Grand Banks. It has a flat bottom with a slight "rocker," or end-to-end curve, and the bottom is both wedge-shaped and narrow. The bow has a long rake to it; the transom is another wedge form.

Dories are notoriously unstable until loaded, and it seems the more you pile on the weight the more stable they become. The sides are angled sharply outward; and the more you add to the boat, the more of the hull is submerged; and the wider it becomes at the waterline. Dories are easily rowed or powered, are displacement hulls basically, but many variations have been developed around the coasts, and some are planing designs.

Catamarans, or twin-hulled boats, were popular a decade or two

*Pontoon boat has twin hulls, is a form of catamaran.*

ago, but are not seen too often today, except in sailing versions. You may see pontoon boats, which are a form of catamaran. In some parts of the country you may occasionally encounter rowing designs that are centuries old; with wine-glass hull cross sections and graceful sterns. They are very popular in the Bahamas as small work and fish boats, sail or power, and with even small outboards they move well.

The study of hull design and development can be an interesting pastime in itself for there are literally hundreds of varieties around the world's waters.

## Types of Boats

### THE "FISHING MACHINE"

The basic boat, of course, is a simple, open hull; a sharpie, dory, skiff, johnboat, or whatever. But when you modify the interior, you begin developing special-purpose craft. A prime example, and a de-

*The "fishing machine" is a sophisticated form of outboard.*

sign that is becoming immensely popular, is the so-called fishing machine. Mention was made earlier of this type.

Hull form is not important—nor is it important in any type discussed here. The adaptation of the "platform" is what counts. The fishing machine is essentially an open boat. The steering station, or console, is usually a little aft of amidships, and on the centerline. You stand up at the helm, as a rule. That means your knees can flex to absorb the shock of pounding in a chop, so you can have the common semi-vee hull with its benefits of shallow draft, stability, and efficiency. Obviously you can also use the deep vee, tri-hull, or whatever.

Fishing machines are exactly that: highly developed and sophisticated boats built for a particular purpose—the pursuit of gamefish, usually in open, coastal waters or other large bodies of water such as the Great Lakes.

They are tough, able, and seakindly. Much fishing gear is built-in, comes with the boat as standard equipment. There are rod racks, under the gun'ls, accommodating four to six or more rods; there are rod holders (not the same thing) that carry rods already rigged and ready for action. Fish boxes, ice chests, bait wells, dry storage, are part of the design. Customarily, there is a short and low bow deck or casting platform forward—with storage underneath.

Any ardent angler would easily love the boat, but they are family craft, too. They can be used for swimming and diving, towing water skiers, camping-cruising, picnics on distant beaches, any form of water activity.

Owners have even made extensive cruises, five hundred miles or more, in such boats. Dry storage is augmented easily (in any boat) by using snap-top, plastic ice chests as "sea chests." Without ice, they can carry clothing and similar gear and keep it dry even in a downpour.

Most, but not all, of these designs are self-bailing. Ship a small sea or a lot of spray, and the water drains out "freeing ports" in the sides or stern. You can leave the boats out all night in a heavy rain—something you can't do with small powerboats that lack self-bailing ability. They can take on enough water, if outboard-types, to submerge the transom motor well, lip and swamp, or sink at the dock. The only alternative is a cockpit cover.

Another form of fishing machine, this one developed largely for calmer, more protected waters, is the "bass boat." It is likely to be a little smaller than the offshore boat, and therefore a tri-hull type with the squared-off bow. There's a slightly easier ride, more room aboard for the length.

Bass boats provide pedestal seats for skipper and fellow angler, although there are variations. The skipper may be well forward, sitting rather high—which means good visibility. Electric "trolling" motors, silent and able to move the boat gently from one good casting spot to another, are fitted on the bow and operated from a foot pedal. The usual storage is provided for rods, ice, bait, and other gear. Some makes have lockable boxes for rods and other valuables.

As with the offshore machine, power can be outboard or sterndrive. A sad commentary on human nature is that buyers sometimes vastly overpower bass boats, especially if they fish in tournaments. Speeds can be sizzling, but unsafe, and efforts are being made to control the situation.

*The bass boat is deservedly popular for inland fishermen.*

Apart from bass boats, there are many other variations intended to appeal to the angler and his family. Most are adaptations of skiffs or tri-hulls, with an operator's seat to starboard, about amidships, room for one or two other anglers, and a few built-in conveniences. They may not offer as much, but they are cheaper to buy, operate, and maintain.

## *THE RUNABOUT*

America's most ubiquitous craft, the runabout, once was virtually the only design available in small powerboats. A decade ago the runabout came in one, unhappy style, featuring a short bow deck at the gun'l level, a windshield, and a fairly large cockpit with seating. It was a lousy fishing boat. You couldn't go forward on the raised bow deck without climbing over or around the windshield, risking a fall overboard. Cockpits tended to become cluttered; the area under the bow deck a rat's nest of miscellany. If you caught a fish, and it began circling the boat, you fell over yourself and others as you moved around to fight it.

You can buy the same configuration today, but it usually has rakish lines, a modified bottom, and is built for speed. Once it was a family boat, used for general purposes. Today it is more or less understood to be for towing waterskiers—at which it shines—or for limited day use, mostly "running about" on lake or bay. In high-performance versions, it can be great sport, and you see people of all ages zipping about in them.

However, the advent of the tri-hull with its extra space forward behind that squared bow brought a new development in runabout design. This is the "bow rider."

Now, bow-riding in a conventional boat, with passengers perched at the stem, legs dangling over the bow, is a dangerous practice that has taken many lives—tragically. Most have been youngsters allowed to bow-ride by indulgent parents.

The bow rider, however, is a different cup of tea. There is a bow compartment, with seating down inside the boat. Access is usually through a "walk-through" windshield. There is more seating in the cockpit, with the operator's station to starboard behind the windshield.

As is the case on most runabouts, storage space is somewhat limited and depends on the ingenuity of designer and builder. The bow-rider boats, however, make excellent all-purpose runabouts with more capacity and versatility than their predecessors.

All boats have canvas options. As an aside, the word "canvas" is still used, even though you never see it in these times when vinyl and other synthetics have taken over.

The bow rider is peculiarly well adapted to the use of "camper covers" which convert the cockpit space into a cozy, waterborne tent. Seats often open up into berths. The boat can be a pleasant cruising craft. Yet it is still relatively small, easily handled, easily trailered. And a point worth noting is that your cruising boat, on the trailer, becomes a mobile home. You can sleep aboard, off the road, while on your way to distant waters for a vacation.

*A conventional runabout, with bow deck and windshield.*

*A modern runabout has bow compartment with seats.*

## *THE WEEKENDER*

This boat is a step up from the runabout. There's a cuddy cabin forward, rather small to be sure, but entirely adequate when you consider the overall length of the boat. Most are still within trailerable limits, a bonus.

With camper covers added at night, the capacity is considerably boosted. Most boats in this class are large enough for little extras, like small galley facilities for cooking. And you are definitely able to add that necessary item, a "head," or marine toilet. Usually they are installed in the cuddy, under the seat-berths.

Weekenders cost more than runabouts, obviously, but offer special satisfactions for the powerboating family that wants to get away from it all for a day or three afloat.

*Camper covers convert boat to overnighter.*

*True weekender has cuddy cabin, other facilities.*

*By carrying a tent along, you can go "boat camping" almost anywhere.*

*Cruising craft are homes afloat.*

## *CRUISING CRAFT*

You are at the upper limits of the "small" powerboat field when you go to a cruising design. That weekender cuddy has grown into a substantial cabin; there may even be a separate, enclosed head compartment; the galley work space is larger, and the berths a bit more comfortable.

It is possible to have full standing headroom, at least in the cockpit under either a hard or soft (convertible) top. No, you cannot live aboard for really extended periods, as you can on the larger designs; but the small cruising craft, up to about 25 feet, has its blessings. It is normally still trailerable, which broadens your cruising horizons; and you don't have the expense of renting a slip to keep the boat in wet storage. Maintenance is obviously reduced.

This "mini-yacht" fills the bill for a small family that enjoys spending a lot of time afloat, whether a weekend or a week at a time. It is entirely adequate despite the small size range, once you learn to limit yourself in the matter of supplies and personal gear.

And there are few pleasures in the world quite so conducive to contentment as rising at dawn, moored in a quiet cove, watching the sun climb over the horizon, listening to fish slap the still waters, and sniffing the heady aroma of coffee coming from the galley.

Small wonder that cruising, as a water sport, has its many adherents.

## *PONTOONS, FLYBRIDGES, AND RACERS*

Don't overlook the pontoon boat, already mentioned. It's really nothing but a platform, but very commodious for the length of the boat. You can buy one complete and ready to accept an outboard motor; or you can buy the pontoons and finish the boat yourself—at a considerable savings.

Pontoons may be plastic, but are more likely to be aluminum. Since they are individually narrow, the boat is easily driven—like displacement hulls. They can plane, however, yielding good speeds.

Pontoon boats, with adequate canvas, make excellent day boats for a family—if used on sheltered waters. They are roomy and comfortable, ideal for a day of picnicking, swimming, anchoring in a cove or off a beach.

Another boat slowly gaining popularity is the "flybridge" or "command bridge" design. At one time this design was limited to large, offshore fishing boats, actually yachts with stiff price tags and operating costs, but adapted to the pursuit of big gamefish. As time passed, however, the advantages of the flybridge intrigued innovative designers and builders, and they began compressing it into smaller hulls. Today you can buy a flybridge boat barely over 20 feet long although usually they are 23 to 25 feet in length.

They are hard to define, which is why the class is listed in this particular grouping. Yes, you can use them for big game fishing, but in all honesty they are not as suitable as the offshore fishing machine properly prepared—and with maybe a small steering tower for more height and better visibility.

*Flybridge boats have cabin below, helm above, make very roomy small cruising craft.*

The flying bridge boats do have fairly cramped cockpits. If you were to catch a sailfish or marlin it would about fill the cockpit. And they are poor fishing boats for smaller species since you can't easily move around the boat. You are forced to troll, a form of angling for which they are ideal since that was the original intent of their larger brethren. You can still fish, but if you catch a big one someone has to be on the flybridge to maneuver the boat, keeping the fish where you want it.

They make excellent weekenders, however, with their cabin accommodations below; and no boat can equal them for visibility from the helm or the delight experienced in steering a course down a broad bay.

High-performance craft may appeal to you. Mention has been made of the zippy style and speeds of some runabouts, but you can find ocean-going speedsters capable of racing offshore, in a fair sea, at 60 miles per hour. It doesn't appeal to everyone, and the prices are extremely high, but open-water racing, in production boats (with modifications by the owner, some of which may bend the rules slightly) has developed a following in the major boating areas such as Florida, New York, the Great Lakes, and California.

There is also small boat racing. Outboard performance class (OPC) racing has thousands of followers in the U.S. They buy stock runabouts, designed for speed afloat, or "tunnel hulls," which are beginning to make their appearance on the regular, pleasure boat market. Tunnel hulls are the descendants of the older catamaran. Take a deep vee hull, split it down the center, swap the two hulls laterally and put them together again. Now you have a hull with an inverted vee section in the middle; a tunnel, which benefits to some degree from aerodynamic lift. A pickle fork tunnel boat—the two hulls stick out separately in front, earning the pickle fork designation—can be extremely fast, even with outboard power. Some have topped a hundred miles per hour!

If you're a boating neophyte, new to the sport, you'll realize there is immense variation within America's recreational navy. Specialization in design has filled the market with choices for anyone, regardless of his interests. Somewhere, there's a boat that will deliver exactly what you expect of it.

*High-performance craft have their own, speedy appeal. This is a "pickle fork" tunnel boat adapted from a racing design.*

*If most of your boating will be done on large open waters, consider a deep vee hull, as it smooths out the bumps.*

## Matching Your Boat to Your Needs

Strange as it may seem, many novice boating families buy the wrong boat. It's a costly error, since the boat becomes "used" the minute you tow it away from the dealer, and you take licking on this instant depreciation. Trading after only a few months can be expensive.

If you are considering buying your first boat, the most important thing you can do is sit down, review the types mentioned earlier, and decide what you want to do with a boat. That's the most important item. Obviously, you wouldn't want a simple, conventional runabout if your primary intent is fishing rather than towing waterskiers. Fit the boat to your planned use of it, rather than the reverse.

That's obvious and needs no elaboration. Less obvious is consideration of the type of water on which you will use the boat. This is where knowledge of hull design becomes valuable.

You shouldn't buy a deep vee hull if your waters are mostly sheltered, often shallow. Gently shelving beaches are also a problem with deep vees, which may draw so much water you ground the boat well off and must wade some distance ashore for picnicking, beachcombing, or whatever. Stick to a shoal draft hull.

But a deep vee underbody is just what the doctor ordered if you live on or near large, open bodies of water that can turn bumpy when the wind's up. Those shoal draft boats with mostly flat bottoms simply can't cope with the chop—sometimes smallish seas—that build up on open water when the wind rises above 15 knots.

An exception might be the fishing machine, where you can stand at the helm to let your knees function as shock absorbers. This is especially true if it has some deadrise (amount of "V") carried to the transom. Otherwise, a deep vee makes exhilarating sport out of running at high speed in bumpy going.

The tri-hull types are a good compromise, which may be why you see so many of them. The more deadrise in a tri-hull, the softer-riding it will be, and the more water it will draw.

As a minor point, deep vees and the high-deadrise tri-hulls are

*Flat-bottom craft are the easiest to beach.*

not as efficient as flatter bottom designs—a fact, already indicated. Roughly, they'll make about 10 percent less speed, on a given amount of power, than a hull with a better planing surface like those semi-vees and skiff types. Or to put it another way, use about 10 percent more fuel for the same speed as a comparable conventional hull.

For this and other reasons, such as superior lateral stability, always try to find the boat with the least amount of deadrise necessary for the waters on which you will use it. Never jump into a deep vee just because it has been heralded as a miracle, a revolution in design. It's all of that, but it isn't perfect.

There just is no such thing as a perfect boat, and never will be. Compromise will always be involved, in both design and selection.

## *ACCOMMODATION SPACE*

Bear this bit of old-salt philosophy in mind: The best boat for anyone is a boat that is just a wee bit too small.

Obviously you want room in a boat; enough room for yourself, your fishing or skiing friends, your family, and all the necessary gear. So, when you eye a boat at a marine dealer's, picture it when all hands are aboard with their rods, tackle, skis, face masks and snorkels, or whatever you know they will bring. Add a mental image of ice chests, the legally required safety equipment, accessories, and other gadgetry you may desire.

Be sure you pick a boat that will take everything aboard without exceeding the safe-load limit. But be wary of anything too large. Prices rise with the square of the boat length, rather than linearly. In other words, a 20-footer can cost a lot more than an 18-footer. Those two extra feet can mean several hundred dollars.

It is better to learn to live within the restrictions imposed by a smaller boat, leaving a lot of unnecessary gear at home. If you want a yacht and can afford it, buy a yacht. If you are entering the world of small powerboats, accept the limitations.

Believe it or not, no boat is ever large enough. You always add extra accessories, accumulate all sorts of junk, just as you do at home. This is why practically everyone inevitably trades up to a larger craft.

Well, if you accept in advance the fact that any boat is going to wind up too small, then you can make good use of the philosophy that the best boat for you is always just a little bit too small. Restrict yourself accordingly, and the money you save can be spent on expanded operations and more fun afloat. Spend your time in active boating, not sweating out heavy monthly payments. Keep your boat as small as possible and live with it.

## *STOWAGE SPACE*

This is where you separate the sheep from the goats. Yes, the best boat for you may be just a wee too small, but an innovative builder who uses his own craft will recognize the limitations and try to make every nook and cranny useful.

When shopping for a boat, pay attention to storage. Look for compartmentation—under berths, if any, under cockpit seating, under the gun'ls, in steering consoles, under bow decks, built in at the transom.

Nothing multiplies the useful dimensions of a small boat more than intelligently planned storage areas. That old-time runabout I mentioned earlier was a real dog in this department. There was no

*Always look for adequate stowage space on any boat.*

place to put anything, and it all wound up under that raised bow deck. In the worst examples, it overflowed into the cockpit and you were forever falling over ice chests and tackle boxes, and stepping on fragile fishing rods.

If you are admiring a small weekender or other cruising-type hull, pay particular attention to the galley (kitchen). It doesn't deserve the name if you can't put things away, even if you live with paper plates and plastic cups.

If you like a boat, are bound and determined to have it, and admit a lack of stowage space, see if you can add to it. I once built a portable galley for a tiny boat. It was a box, with hinged cover, that opened onto braces to form a shelf. Two Sterno stoves went on the opened cover, and I could fish out food items, eating utensils, and small pots and pans from the depths of the box.

On a boat I own today I have a "gear locker" which is nothing but a wooden box, with fiberglassed edges (to make it watertight). It's painted a nautical blue, has golden nylon rope handles, took a few hours to make. It fits under a cockpit seat and holds loose gear that should be readily at hand—docklines, fenders, a couple of life jackets, horn, anchor and line, and other oddments. Saves a lot of lost time fishing around in the small cabin.

Consider stowage space. It's at a premium on small boats. And if you can't see a way to improve it by building your own additions, the boat may turn out to be an unwise choice. You can't enjoy going to sea in a floating trash dump, knee-deep in all your gear.

## *CAN YOU FIX EVERYTHING?*

Ease of repair and maintenance is a vital point to consider when selecting a boat. Things do break, fail, and malfunction, and not necessarily because of manufacturing defects. Neglect can do a lot of damage; so can sloppy docking maneuvers.

Can you fix everything? It's not going to seem like an important matter if you bump against a pier and knock off a stern cleat. Cleats aren't expensive. But if you can't get under the gun'l to hold the nuts so you can bolt on a replacement, you're in for a costly repair job. And cleats must be bolted down, with a backing plate underneath the gun'l. Common screws cannot hold a cleat for long, considering the stresses they must withstand. This is as good a time as any to mention that people have been killed when cleats tore out and a towline snapped back.

If you can't fix a cleat properly, you are probably the victim of a boatbuilder who erroneously assumes his boat will remain in perfect condition through all eternity. The same thing goes for other hardware, lights, and the important fuel and electrical systems—which will be treated in more detail next.

# *FUEL AND ELECTRICAL SYSTEMS TO CONSIDER*

## *Fuel Systems*

The smaller outboard boat has no fuel system to speak of. One or more portable fuel tanks, usually six-gallon capacity, carry the fuel; a flexible hose is employed to connect the tank in use to the engine. As

*Small boats may get by with only portable tanks.*

long as they are not stored in enclosed spaces where fumes can accumulate, creating the hazard of potential fire or even explosion, the system is eminently safe. All you have to do is regularly check the tanks for leaks and rusted edges on the bottom—a common occurrence, in time, on metallic tanks—and watch the hoses. They do wear, can crack, may require replacement.

Larger outboards and sterndrive boats usually have built-in tanks, and the system itself is more complex. Let's take them in order.

## *FUEL TANKS*

Larger fuel tanks are apt to contain any of a variety of materials. Common even today is terneplate, steel with a thin coating of lead. You'll probably find a terneplate tank on your auto. It has the advantage of being cheap and easily formed, which is why it is so common. Nearly all portable outboard tanks are terneplate.

However, terneplate has several major disadvantages. When the protective coating begins to wear away, exposing the bare metal, the tank starts to rust. Rusting and corrosion start quickly on the bottom edges, exposed to water, and pinhole leaks can develop. Terneplate tanks just don't last long. Even portables, if exposed regularly to salt water, may start leaking in just a few years.

When you install a larger terneplate tank in the bilges, below decks, its life may be even further shortened. Sitting constantly in a tiny puddle of bilge water significantly reduces its life. For this reason the government is taking a long, hard look at terneplate. In time, its use may be outlawed, though perhaps only in permanent installations.

Many boatbuilders started some years ago using aluminum tanks. Aluminum can't rust and a well-made tank of this material will far outlast terneplate. Aluminum in thinner gauges, however, can't pass the fire tests. Yes, tanks made by responsible manufacturers must withstand rigid tests including exposure to fire. Terneplate can stand up, but aluminum has a lower melting point. In heavier gauges, and especially if covered with a fire-retardant paint, aluminum is entirely adequate. It's a better choice by far than terneplate, anyway.

You may occasionally see galvanized tanks, although they are fading from the small powerboat scene. Like terneplate, they are low in cost. But in the construction process some of the zinc coating is eroded at the seams, and they don't last much longer than terneplate.

A few stock boatbuilders offer fiberglass tanks, usually in below-deck installations. If made with fire-retardant resin, by a responsible manufacturer, they are fine tanks. They do not rust or corrode, can last many years, and aren't bothered by sitting in bilge water.

The problem with fiberglass tanks is their lack of opacity, even when the resin has been pigmented. The sun can shine through the sides of the tank, hastening oxidation and deterioration of the fuel. So they should not be used above the decks, in what are called "saddle" tank configuration—under the gun'ls.

There are other materials the average small boat buyer would probably never encounter. Black iron is used extensively for diesel fuel tanks. Stainless steel has some use, but isn't popular—partly because of cost. There's also the belief that stainless is more responsive to temperature changes, and more likely to foster condensation of atmospheric water inside the tank—leading to water in the gas and engine problems.

Most costly of all is Monel, an almost indestructible nickel-copper alloy. You may find it on yachts, but a Monel tank on the average small powerboat could cost $400 or more, which effectively rules it out.

That leaves us with terneplate, aluminum, and fiberglass. Terneplate should never be used in the bilges, below decks; fiberglass should never be used above decks, exposed to sunlight; aluminum can go in any area, but should be heavy-gauge metal (most are) and coated with fire-resistant paint (few are).

## *FUEL TANK INSTALLATIONS*

Permanent fuel tanks should be installed with some attention to reasonable, industry standards. You can save a lot of checking if you look for the Boating Industry Association (BIA) certification. BIA engineers check out installations "on the line" at boatbuilding firms and certify that the systems are up to snuff.

If there is no BIA plate on the fuel system, you should know certain basics. Tanks should not have lips or rims around the top—which can trap water, accelerating deterioration. They should be firmly supported underneath, with good air circulation around them, and not just sitting in the bilges. No padding should be used on the supports, since the blotter-like action can keep them damp, and the last thing you want is constant dampness on a tank.

Tanks should be well secured, not likely to move around in a sea. Unhappily, too many builders in the past decade have been meeting this standard by foaming their tanks in place below decks. Expanding polyurethane foam, mixed and poured (or sometimes sprayed) in place can, when it sets, lock a tank in place so it wouldn't budge if you dropped the boat off a building. This makes it impossible to easily examine the tank, in a periodic maintenance inspection. Foamed-in tanks, especially when sealed under a deck or cockpit sole, can develop unsuspected leaks and eventually lead to fire or worse.

Gradual recognition of problems of fuel tank installation has led to some ingenious solutions, and also some halfway measures that do provide a compromise:

1. The tank may be fiberglass, much less likely to develop leaks—if well made to begin with. It won't rust, rot, or corrode. Baffling (the inside of a tank must have some means to keep gasoline from sloshing back and forth) may be a form of foam long used in racing cars. It holds the fuel like a sponge, but still permits it to flow.

2. Tanks may be only partially foamed in place, usually with the foam under the tank and partway up the sides, but not covering the top—so you can inspect the fittings and fuel lines. (You still can't see the bottom edges, however, and removing the tank for a thorough examination is all but impossible. The foam is like cement, and must all be laboriously chipped away, even with the aid of solvents.)

3. Rather than a sealed tank under the deck, a common installation on smaller powerboats, there may be a large, screwed-down deck panel over the tank. It is the buyer's responsibility to take it up periodically—and laboriously—so the tank can be checked. In any case, there should at least be an inspection and access hatch, so you can examine and maintain the fittings and lines.

Any boat with a totally inaccessible fuel tank, where you can't even see the lines, connections, and other gadgetry, can be unsafe. And once you've bought one (and found that your insurance company won't give you any insurance), it's too late to do anything about it.

*Fuel fills should be on side decks.*

## *FUEL FILL LINES*

The deck fill should be on the side deck, covering board, or gun'l, outside the cockpit. It should not be so located that spillage will wind up inside the boat, creating hazardous fumes.

The only permissible exception would be those few models of outboard "fishing machines" with fuel fills on the center console, feeding a tank below. If self-bailing, and most are with this arrangement, fuel spillage has no place to go; fumes can't accumulate. All you have to do is wipe up the spilled gas. (Don't hose it out the freeing ports. It's against the law to spill any oily product overside, even so small an amount that it causes only a slight sheen on the water.)

The fuel deck fill is connected to the tank by a flexible hose. There must be an electrical continuity, which usually is provided by a hose made of a conducting material. If the hose can't ground to the tank, then a wire should be included. The idea is to prevent static sparks—which obviously can be unsafe.

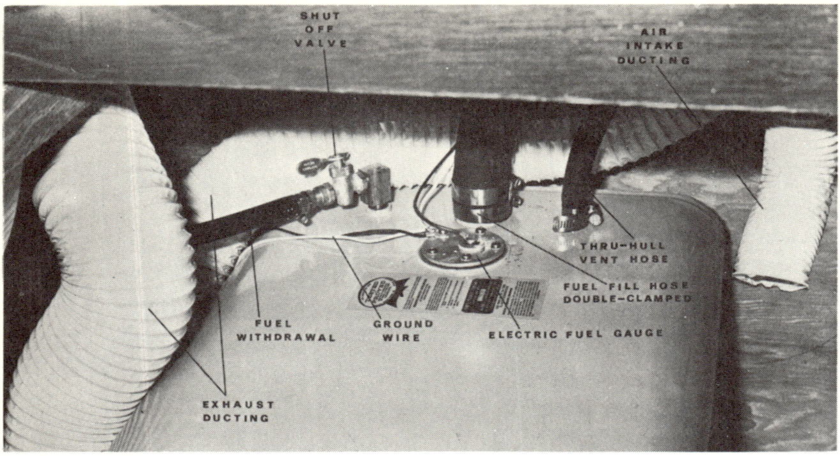


*Good permanent installation follows safety standards with grounding, shut-off valve, proper ventilation of area.*

Clamps hold the hose at the deck fill and tank. They should be stainless steel. Double-clamping is a guarantee of longer life. And the clamps should be accessible. Be wary of boats where you can't get at the clamp connection to replace a worn, loose unit.

On most small boats the pick-up hose leading to the engine is also flexible. It may be copper tubing. If it is, the last few inches between copper line and engine must be flexible to isolate vibration.

Somewhere in the system there should be a shut-off valve. You should be able to shut off the fuel flow, at the tank. If you see a shut-off in the engine compartment or box of a sterndrive boat, that's strictly a "service" shut-off for the benefit of a mechanic working on the engine.

Why a tank shut-off? Because on most boats the fuel line may droop below the tank, on its path to the engine. In the event of a broken line the gasoline may siphon out of the tank and into the bilges. A fuel shut-off valve will stop it. So will a gadget called an "anti-siphon" valve, but few are found on small powerboats. Federal regulations may one day require them. There's nothing funny about a deep puddle of gasoline in the bilges.

Distribution lines should be linked to the common ground for safety. This is why, when a tank is filled, the pump nozzle should be touched to the side of the deck fill. You ground it, and prevent a static electricity spark.

## *COMPARTMENT VENTILATION*

Any time you put a fuel tank in a closed compartment, it must be ventilated. You've got to have air flowing through it to pick up and dispel any slight amount of fumes that may gather. This is done with cowls mounted on the decks or transom, connected to fairly large ducts leading into and out of the compartment. The intake duct must extend halfway to the bilges, or at least below the level of the carburetor air intake. The exhaust duct must go all the way to the bilges or bottom of the compartment.

When the boat is moving, air will flow into the upper part of the fuel compartment. It will "scavenge" the fumes—if any—and the exhaust duct will pick them up at the bottom, carrying them out of the boat.

*Fuel compartments must have air vents linked to proper ducting below.*

Little things, like a smooth laminar flow of air, can be important. There should be no obstructions blocking the ducts. What you want is a ventilation system that will pour air into the fuel compartment and then draw it out again, carrying fumes with it. An intake duct on a side deck, with a smooth length of clear deck ahead of it, will function better than one on a transom, where there would be air turbulence.

No ventilation systems are required on fuel systems in which the tank is not enclosed. You will see some small boats with built-in tanks where the bulkheading is open at the bottom. Technically, it is not a closed compartment and therefore no ventilation is needed.

Note: If you stick a small, portable, six-gallon outboard tank in a locker of any kind, where it is enclosed, it should be ventilated. At the very least, lack of ventilation will earn a reprimand or stern look from a Coast Guard boarding officer.

And one more comment, fortunately affecting very few buyers of small powerboats. Try to avoid side or updraft carburetors—which you will find only on a few four-cycle engines. They should be fitted with drip pans, and if they lack them, they aren't safe—for obvious reasons. Downdraft carbs are far safer, and need no means to collect drippings.

In summation, if you buy any boat large enough to have a permanently installed fuel system, make sure it is a safe one and that you can get at the system periodically to inspect the components and maintain or replace them.

The trouble with modern fiberglass boats is that they can outlive a succession of owners, but fuel systems may need replacement from time to time.

## *Electrical Systems*

### *BATTERIES*

The heart of any electrical system is the battery. It should be in a dry location, above the bilges, well secured against movement and shock, and covered. To meet all these desirable standards, small boat batteries are often enclosed in fiberglass boxes.

The reasons for keeping batteries secure and out of bilge water are obvious. You also keep them covered—especially when they are installed in the engine compartment or box of a sterndrive boat—because dropping a tool across the terminals can cause a spark. If that spark should occur while you're working on a leaky fuel line, you might be involved in a serious accident.

It is desirable, on more complex installations with a lot of electronic and electrical gadgetry aboard, to have a main shut-off switch. You can disconnect the battery when the boat is not in use. It prevents slow discharge and a phenomenon called stray current electrolysis, which will be taken up later.

## *WIRING*

Small outboards and sterndrives usually have very simple electrical systems. You may only have a couple of navigation lights, apart from the engine's electrical starter and generator. In such cases, they may be fed by wiring directly from the battery, with in-line fuses for protection. Just be sure you can get at the wiring for maintenance.

Larger outboards and sterndrives will have more complex systems. In addition to navigation lights, they may have cabin and cockpit lights, radios, depth sounders, and other gadgetry.

It is customary to install a fused terminal board at some convenient location. Heavy-gauge wires from the battery feed the terminals, to which you connect everything else.

The first thing you should do when buying a boat is be certain you can get at the terminal board! Some builders seem to take a perverse delight in installing them behind bulkheads, often with covers screwed down over them. If a navigation light fuse blows at 2 A.M. you must first find a screwdriver, then take the cover off, then try to change the fuse—if you remember where you kept the spares.

Very often the design of a boat will reflect the fact that the builder has experienced an electrical problem after midnight. Everything is accessible. Some boats will have external fusing, with caps at the dashboard. Just pull the cap and change the fuse. Delightful.

Also, when checking a boat before buying, make sure the terminal board has room for additional wiring. You may want to add a radio and other devices. There should be spare hookups.

Boats aren't like autos, in which the frame serves as a ground return. Boats have two-wire systems, and on nearly all boats it is a grounded system, and negative ground at that. Yellow is the color for negative, red or black wire is used for the "hot" or positive side. If you add anything yourself, stick to the color code. Peeking under the dash of a new boat is a good way to check the builder's attention to detail. A rat's nest of wires, with no apparent effort to maintain a color code, reveals sloppy workmanship.

Look at the lugs on the ends of the wires. There are the round or U-shaped ends, crimped to the bared wire tips, which go on the terminal posts. They constitute one of the biggest weaknesses in powerboating. An astonishing number of builders fail to appreciate what can happen when you pair up dissimilar metals, and then ask them to cooperate in a marine atmosphere.

This digression is important, since we'll be talking about it at length later on. If you stick two dissimilar metals into an electrolytic solution (like salt water) you have created a battery. A weak current will flow from one of the metals—the weaker one on the galvanic scale. In the process the weaker metal will erode. In this manner lugs that are not compatible with the wiring can cause electrolysis and subsequent circuit failure. You may have to remove the lug from the terminal board, clip the wire shorter, and put a new lug on.

Cheap dimestore-type electrical lugs don't belong on boats. And you won't find them on better craft.

A whole book could be written about low-voltage systems on boats; the interested amateur can find such a book, if he wants more detail. Only the brief basics were outlined here to help you buy a better boat. To summarize my own advice, make sure you can get at every component in your electrical system—and that includes the battery, which some builders will hide behind bulkheads so you can't easily check them for charge level. And make sure the wiring is neatly installed, secured, and protected from chafing or wear—anytime it passes through a bulkhead, for example, it should go through a soft grommet so it can't abrade. A good system may be complex but it is also easy to get at and understand, easily maintained.

*Side decks should permit going forward safely, easily.*

# CONSTRUCTION FACTORS TO CONSIDER

## Safety Features

We've already mentioned the value of flotation, and the advantages of self-bailing cockpits. A few other factors should be borne in mind. You want non-skid surfaces on decks, to lessen the chances of slipping overboard. Decks do get wet. Side decks on cabin craft should be wide enough to permit going forward handily to take care of the anchor or dock lines. A toe rail along the edge is desirable. It can keep your feet from slipping overside. Grab rails on cabin sides are also helpful. An old rule of the sea is, "one hand for the ship, one hand for yourself," and grab rails at strategic locations make things a good deal safer.

Be wary of boats with lots of sharp, hard corners on the inside, where you can bang yourself badly when you lurch. It's rare, but occasionally you see a boat with a poorly designed companionway, for example, where you could get hurt.

This is also the time to mention devices called "through hull fittings." You don't find them on most small powerboats, unless there is a toilet, with outside discharge – not very likely in these days, as some laws require holding tank systems. Through hull fittings are necessary on inboards, for cooling water intakes. On good boats, any such fitting will be equipped with a seacock, usually in the form of a gate valve. (Good, bronze seacocks wholesale at around $70, which is why most builders substitute cheaper gate valves.)

You see, the cooling water intake is fed to the engine via a hose,

*The "boat" in this photo is only the inner liner part. With engine added, it runs safely, can't sink, even though it lacks the outer hull. Good boats are safe boats.*

clamped to the engine intake and to the hull fitting. Clamps can give way, water can flood the hull. You want a valve to turn it off for safety's sake. Lacking a valve, you as the owner will have to take the responsibility of obtaining tapered wooden plugs that can be driven into the fitting to halt the inrushing water. Boats have sunk because a tiny, cheap clamp gave way and there was no way to shut off the water flow.

The odds are that you'll never see a through hull fitting on a new, small powerboat, since discharging toilets are on the way out. If you do see one, however, make sure you can get at it easily and quickly, and have some way to shut off the water flow.

On cabin craft, it is also nice to have access to the bilges forward. Sometimes boats at rest float slightly bow down, and bilge water can flow forward to just lay there. You can't pump the bilges dry unless you can get at that forward area. And if you were unlucky enough (and careless enough) to hole the hull forward in a collision, you might jolly well wish you could get into the bilges. On some boats you can't.

A last word about cabin craft. Industry standards call for a secondary means of egress from cabins, meaning in plain English an "escape hatch." You wouldn't want a house with only one door. And you shouldn't buy a boat with only one companionway leading to the cabin. There should be another means of exit—just in case.

If all of this talk makes boating sound unsafe, please be assured that such is not the case. Most accidents are caused by operator error or faulty judgment. The idea behind having a boat built to proper standards is to make the equipment as safe as possible. The rest is up to the owner-skipper. Boating can be very safe indeed. But it pays in any game you play to have the best possible equipment.

## *Judging a Fiberglass Hull*

The most popular type of construction today is fiberglass. And the most popular form of judging quality in construction is to thump the hull smartly with the fist. It's about as effective as tire kicking in a used car lot. Go ahead and thump. Everyone does. If your fist goes through the hull, obviously it's paper-thin. Usually, even on poor boats, they use enough glass and resin to provide a sound skin.

In fact, some cheapie boats may even have more glass than a more costly boat. The inexpert builder doesn't always trust himself, and may use more raw material than he really needs. Thump away, but use these guidelines for judging construction quality:

1. Kneel down at an angle to the boat so you can see reflections in the side, as if you were looking toward a mirror. Those reflected images should not be badly mottled and distorted. The key word is "badly." There'll be some distortion on any boat. But on poor hulls, it is so obvious it almost kicks you in the teeth and shouts, "Look at me, I'm a ba-a-ad boat!"

2. Kneel down forward and aft of the boat and try to judge the fairness of the longitudinal lines. They should be straight and true, not wobbly, wavy or crooked. Keel, chines, risers if any, shouldn't look like a Scottish walking stick.

*Get down and examine reflections in the sides of the boat.*

3. Examine any area where fiberglass turns a sharp corner. Look for checking—hairline cracks and crazing. The radii of corners should be easy with fiberglass, which doesn't like sharp turns. Smart designers and builders know this, and you won't find cracked corners on their boats.

4. Check sub-assemblies for quality and workmanship. This would include hatches, which should be well built, not poorly molded and carelessly sawed to fit, and windshields, which should be well made and securely installed, not shaky and loose.

These four tests alone separate the sheep from the goats speedily, and you don't have to be a 24-karat expert to apply them.

On any boat, built of any material, check the hardware. Cleats are supposed to be bolted through the decks, not just screwed in place. And they are supposed to be backed up underneath. Ditto bow rails, stern rails, and grab rails. Hardware should be good quality, of adequate size, not flaky, peeling, or tiny.

A word about aluminum: lines should be fair and true. If welded, there should be no distortion in the skin from the welding process. Aluminum should be heavy gauge.

Any boat needs internal support, usually in the form of longitudinal stringers. In glass boats they may be wood, and if they are they should be completely "encapsulated" or covered with fiberglass. You'll have to take the salesman's word on this, since you can't get at the stringers in many boats. Bare wood stringers can rot out. They won't if encapsulated; and if the wood does rot eventually it isn't important, because the glass "girder" remains. On better glass boats, stringers are all glass, separately molded and then bonded in the boat's bottom, often in a "hat" cross section.

## *Steering and Controls*

Nearly all small powerboats nowadays steer with what is termed cable, or "push-pull" systems. There's a heavy cable inside a flexible tube. A fitting at one end goes to the outboard or sterndrive engine (or inboard rudder quadrant). The other end is geared to the wheel.

The push-pull cable can be moved back and forth inside its housing, transmitting the motion of the helm to the engine or rudder. It's like the old Bowden wire, used as a manual choke control years ago. The housing can be bent around easy curves, which means such a steering system is simple to install, positive-acting, and vastly superior to the old drum-and-cable types.

Gearing designs differ. One unit has a simple worm gear operating on a helical cable. Another type has a pinion gear working on the inner face of an internal ring gear attached to a drum to which the steering cable is attached. Probably best of all is the rack and pinion type. A pinion gear at the wheel moves a bar, with gear teeth on one edge, and the bar provides a positive connection to the cable.

Rack and pinion steering is sturdy and durable, but bulkier than the others, and the end of the rack-gear housing may protrude out the side of the helm console on some boats. It's very strong, however, and has another advantage. You can double up on it, installing another rack linked to a second cable on the opposite side of the boat. It's almost a must if you buy a boat with dual, big sterndrives. You can pull easier than you can push, and the doubled steering linkage allows you to handle two engines with far more ease. On simpler boats with smaller duals, one cable and a tie-rod to the second engine usually suffices.

Really big sterndrive engines in pairs usually require power steering—expensive, and sometimes delicate—and in most cases if the power unit breaks down it takes a gorilla to steer the boat.

The better steering systems have grease fittings near the engine linkage so they can be lubricated. Lack of use and insufficient lubrication mean a frozen cable. The only way to get it loose is to rap the end of the linkage with a rubber or plastic mallet. Be wary of stickiness in new steering. It can mean a cable bent so sharply that it will cause trouble sooner or later. Steering should be easy and effortless.

There are hydraulic steering systems. In these, a pump which is linked to the wheel pressurizes an oil-line when the wheel is turned, and actuates the steering linkage. Efforts have been made to utilize plastic tubing for the lines, adapting hydraulic systems for small powerboats, but at this writing they were far from perfected. Most hydraulic systems still use copper hydraulic lines and their use is confined to somewhat larger craft.

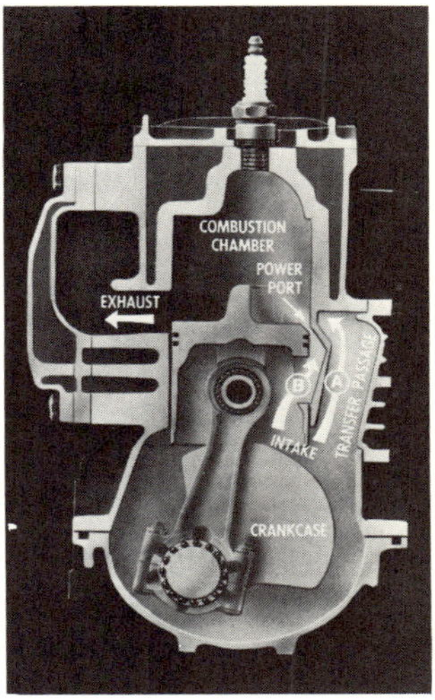


Left: *The outboard engine is the most popular form of propulsion.* Right: *The 2-cycle engine lacks valves. Fuel charge and exhaust move via ports in cylinder walls.*

# POWER OPTIONS TO CONSIDER

## *Types of Engines*

### *TWO-CYCLE OUTBOARDS*

This is not an essay on engines, with which most American males have a natural affinity anyway. However, some explanation is due the neophyte, since differing engine types are important in marine applications.

The two-stroke engine delivers power on every other movement of the piston in the cylinder, on every "second" stroke.

Every time the piston rises in the cylinder, it compresses a fuel charge which ignites, driving the piston down on a power stroke. There are no valves. The fuel-air mixture enters the cylinder through a port in the wall, exposed when the piston is down. The exhaust goes out another port, similarly exposed. Fresh fuel pushes the burned charge out—and some escapes with the gases, which is why two-cycles consume more fuel than comparable four-cycle engines. Some is wasted. Careful design of the piston's top surface minimizes the loss.

Two-stroke engines have fewer moving parts, are simple, extremely durable, and promise a long life of service with minimal wear. Maintenance is usually easy. Oil is mixed with the gasoline to provide lubrication.

## *FOUR-CYCLE STERNDRIVES*

In these engines, only one piston stroke out of every four produces power. The piston first compresses the fuel-air mixture, which is ignited to produce a downward power stroke. That's two strokes. But there are two more: one upward stroke to push the burned gases out an exhaust valve and one more downward stroke to admit a fresh charge of fuel through an intake valve. Then comes the compression stroke to begin another cycle.

With four-stroke design, the exhaust gases are completely scavenged. Fresh fuel is not wasted. Four-stroke mills are thus more efficient than two-cycle engines.

But the four-bangers are more complex, have valves that may need attention from time to time. Oil is pumped from the crankcase to provide lubrication, and it adds to the complexity. Four-stroke engines are also heavier than outboards. The weight-to-horsepower ratio is higher. And they just can't take the abuse you can dish out to a two-banger.

## *WHICH ENGINE TO CHOOSE*

Quite a few boats are offered on the market with a choice of power left up to the buyer. You can have an inboard (usually as a sterndrive) or an outboard. Which is right?

On smaller hulls, the outboard is an obvious choice. It is lighter in weight, delivers more power per pound, is easier to care for, and requires little attention. Substitute a far heavier four-cycle engine in the same boat, and the increase in weight pulls the speed down. In terms of miles per gallon, the four-cycle engine is no more economical. I've tested similar hulls, with each type of engine, and found the difference in miles per gallon to be insignificant.

Go to a larger hull and you may be happier with a sterndrive. It can provide more power, the bigger hull can easily carry the extra weight, and economy becomes more important because fuel savings can be significant.

*The sterndrive has an inboard four-cycle engine and through-the-transom outboard drive. Like the outboard, it can tilt up and is easy to beach.*

If you want a rule of thumb, this is it: Opt for the outboard anytime the available power, in single- or dual-engine installations, can easily move the boat at a moderate cruising speed. Outboards are definitely not gas hogs when throttled well back, with enough reserve power to shove a hull easily without lugging, or the boat squatting and falling off plane. Outboarding, however, can be costly if you have to run at full throttle all the time to keep the boat on plane and running smoothly. On larger, heavier hulls, consider the sterndrive. But bear in mind they have more hardware, therefore require more attention and maintenance, and can be somewhat more sensitive than the durable old kicker.

## *ROTARIES, TURBINES, JETS, AND INBOARDS*

You can probably buy a Wankel outboard. Smaller versions are manufactured in Italy and Japan. At this writing there is one American manufacturer of Wankel outboard engine prototypes for racing boats, and they might be marketed in a year or two. The rotary engine does show promise. It has also been hooked up to sterndrive lower units and tested extensively as an inboard in larger craft.

The supreme advantage of the rotary is its simplicity and capacity to run literally forever, at high speed, with little need for maintenance. It is also extremely smooth running, with no vibration. But the rotary engine, at least right now, is very expensive, and no manufacturer is tooled up to make it in quantity. It also uses a lot of fuel, and the exhaust is dirty, although easily cleaned up. We may be on the edge of a Wankel age in the marine world, but it shows few signs of booming suddenly.

As for turbines, they've been tried in boats as small as 20 feet. But they are far too costly, and too delicate, and some very expensive experiments went down the drain when they tried to adapt them to pleasure craft.

This is as good a time as any to bring up the subject of water jet propulsion. Jet drives were invented in 1960 by a New Zealander. Their first appearance in the U.S. was a marketing disaster. In recent years, however, they seem to have been making a comeback.

*The Wankel-type rotary outboard is being tested on raceboats.*

The idea is not new. Even Ben Franklin suggested in print that a water jet would propel a boat better than paddlewheels. The theory is fine. A pump in the boat, which may be centrifugal or axial flow, or both, draws in water from a grilled intake in the boat bottom and ejects it from a discharge in the transom. The boat obeys Newton's Third Law of Motion—for every action there is an equal and opposite reaction—and moves forward. But it never worked until they raised the water jet discharge so it was above the surface. Submerged jets failed.

Early jets lacked the capacity to move a lot of water, and so develop little thrust. Also, the intakes were easily clogged by weeds. Today's jet engines are far superior, more powerful due to having more efficient pumps, and the intakes are less easily clogged. Also, they've added access ports so you can open up an intake and clean it out.

Jet boats are lively, with jackrabbit acceleration, and are highly maneuverable. They reverse with a gate, like the "clamshells" used on jet aircraft to reverse the thrust when they land. With a jet you can go from full speed ahead to full speed reverse without tossing shredded gear teeth all over the seascape. Also, there is no whirling propeller, which could injure skiers or divers. Jets are safer boats. Of course their most obvious advantage is that you can run them in extremely shallow water, and if you should go hard aground, you won't tear up a lot of underbody hardware.

On the debit side, they gulp gas at low speeds and are not really efficient until the boat is up on plane and running easily. They should never be installed on larger hulls of the semi-planing or displacement varieties, not unless you own you own gasoline refinery. And they should never be installed on boats kept in wet storage afloat on the coasts. Barnacles can grow on the interior of the intake and even on the blades of the pump.

Inboards were saved for last, because you see relatively few of them on smaller hulls. They do have all the benefits of the four-cycle engine, yet none of the complexities of the sterndrive. Underbody hardware is simple. The boats can be kept in wet storage, whereas you invite disaster if you try this with a sterndrive engine, with its lower unit constantly submerged. Electrolysis, and subsequent deterioration, are certain.

You do see some "vee-drive" inboards. The engines are set aft, and the shafts are extended forward to gear boxes, from which the propeller shafts are reversed to run aft under the boat. Vee drives save a lot of space, but careful alignment is a must, and only a handful of builders have the expertise to work up a proper installation. Vee drives are at their best on houseboats, where you see growing numbers of them.

## *Buy Enough Power*

The worst mistake anyone can make is to underpower a boat. The average marine engine has it hard enough as it is. Unlike autos, where the engine can push a car 50 or more miles per hour yet still be loafing, a boat engine works all the time.

To prevent the poor bit of iron from total collapse, allow a little leeway on power. Buy the biggest engine you can afford, consistent with safety. There's no law saying you have to run at full throttle all the time. Throttle back, and a big engine can loaf just a little, like an auto engine, and will respond to this kind treatment by staying healthy.

How much power do you need? Fortunately, you can figure it out in advance from a simple weight-to-horsepower ratio. It's all done for you on the accompanying nomogram, which is a "slideless" slide rule tailored to a specific computation.

You can even carry the rule around with you in your head, if you can remember the magic numbers, "30-30." Think of the old-time deer hunter's beloved "thutty-thutty" and you've got it fixed in your mind. The average boat with an efficient bottom needs one horsepower to move each 30 pounds of weight at a speed of 30 miles per hour. Thirty pounds per horse equals 30 miles per hour. It's that simple.

For each change in weight of three pounds, speed will vary inversely by two miles per hour. In other words, add three pounds to your one horse, speed drops two miles per hour. Take away three pounds, speed rises two miles per hour.

Suppose you are buying an outboard and want some idea of how it will perform with a given engine. First, total up the gross weight: hull weight, engine weight, fuel load (gasoline weight is six pounds per gallon), people-load, extra equipment, and gear. Then divide this figure by the horsepower. Use the manufacturer's stated horsepower (an allowance has been made for this, and the fact that enginemakers sometimes are a little enthusiastic about the actual horsepower involved).

This gives you the weight-to-horsepower ratio. If it is 30:1, you can expect 30 miles per hour from an average, conventional planing hull; and about 10 percent less for deep vees and extreme tri-hulls.

If the ratio is 33:1, expect a top speed at full throttle of about 28. Use the nomogram—it's easier. But carry the rule around in your head. You'd be amazed how well it works. You can inquire of boating friends what their boats weigh, work out the formula roughly in your head, and tell them their top speed. Conversely, you can take a known speed and horsepower, and compute approximate weight.

*Use this nomogram to predict speed from given boat/motor combination: Using any straightedge, connect the gross weight of your fully loaded boat (left scale) with its total horsepower (right scale). Read the expectable speed where the straightedge intersects the center scale.*

*Most boats achieve 90 percent or more of the nomogram speed. A few exceed it. Anything less than 90 percent could mean problems, such as inefficient hull or poor trim.*

WEIGHT/HORSEPOWER SPEED NOMOGRAM

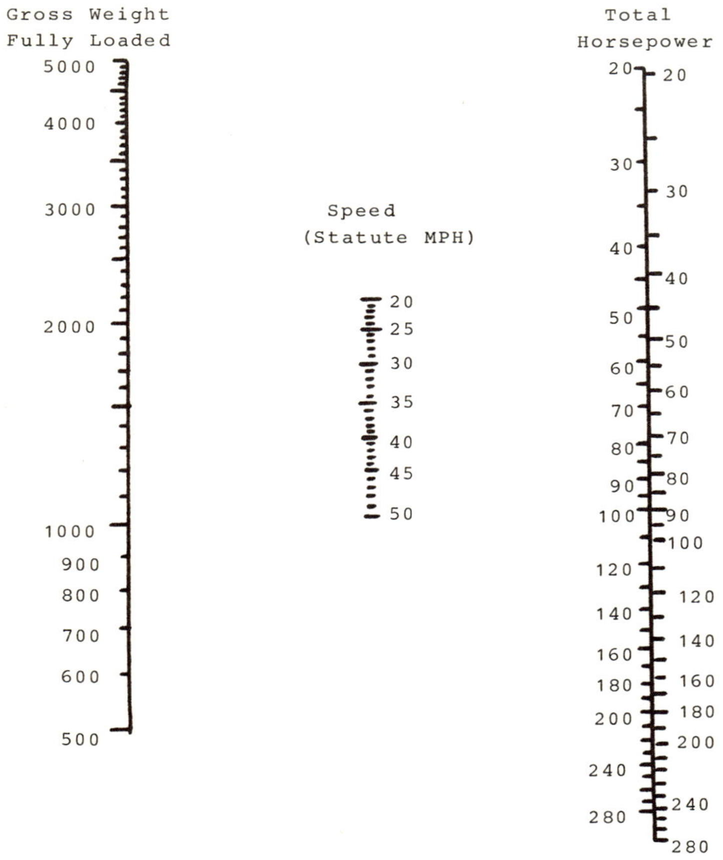

With the formula and/or nomogram, you can estimate in advance what you want, and power your boat to produce that desired performance. I'd suggest, for most outboards and sterndrives, a desirable top speed of 35 miles per hour, knowing that you will ease back and cruise at, say, 25 to 30 when wind and water conditions permit. Knowing the interrelation of weight and power helps you avoid later overloading of a boat. Load factors are important, and can ruin a hull's performance.

Apart from sluggish performance, heavily loaded and underpowered boats lose seakindliness and are a pure pain in the neck. Correlate the horsepower and gross load with earlier selection factors relating to capacity, and you will be a lot happier with your boat than the guy who took potluck at the dealer's, pointing to a shiny new hull and announcing, "I'll take that one."

Figure these things out in advance. You'll be a happier skipper, with a more contented crew. And the engine will last longer, too.

## *One Engine or Two?*

There's one argument you'll hear on every waterfront, with salty old veterans just as positive in conflict with each other as they are with novices: Which is better? One main engine on an outboard hull, with a tiny spare kicker for emergency get-home power in case of a breakdown, or dual engines of the same power?

There are advantages to both, of course. One big engine costs less than two of only slightly less power. You can add a spare kicker of about 10 horsepower, for insurance, and still come out with a smaller investment. But dual, matched engines mean plenty of reserve power should one of them fail, and losing both is unheard of since you can always cannibalize the ailing mill for parts to keep its twin brother perking along.

The answer is quite simple, really. Your choice depends on the type of water on which you'll do most of your boating. If it will be mostly on protected, inland waters, where a mild chop is the worst you may expect and winds rarely reach brisk levels, go for the main-

*If you fish far offshore, as are these anglers working near an oil rig, install dual, matched outboards.*

engine-and-small-spare philosophy. If the big engine quits on you, the little one on a transom bracket will get you back to the dock.

But if you operate on big water, open bays and sounds, or even short distances offshore in the sea, then forget the spare-kicker concept. Go for matched, dual engines. The reason is that tiny kickers can't push a larger hull against wind and sea. Quite a few people who put their faith in the less costly notion of spare kickers find this out the hard way. You can't make a decent speed with a small engine on a bigger boat. If it's rough, you may not make any headway at all. This is when you want duals. If one fails, the other will move you back to the dock. It may still be a slow journey—you probably won't have enough power to get the boat on plane—but at least you'll beat the wind and sea conditions, and make hull speed (explained earlier).

It's true that you won't get as much speed from twin 50-horsepower outboards as you will from a single 100-horsepower engine. Two kickers have a bit more underwater drag. But the difference is only a few percentage points, nothing to worry about. And a 50-horse mill can really push a boat, when its brother fails.

Go for duals on big water. Choose the big single with back-up spare kicker only on smaller hulls, and more protected waters.

*If you stay in protected waters, go for one main engine and a spare kicker on a retractable bracket.*

## How Much Fuel Will You Burn?

Until recent years, nobody, but nobody, who could afford any boat ever fretted about fuel. Now all hands want to have some idea of how much gasoline a boat will consume.

Luckily, that handy computing digit—the thumb—can serve again. As a rough rule, gas engines burn about one gallon per hour for each 10 horsepower. It varies slightly between two- and four-cycle engines.

How to economize on fuel is a subject that will come later. If you want to obtain a fairly close estimate on probable fuel use, use the accompanying nomogram. I developed it empirically from years of testing boats, hooking up fuel-flow meters, and plotting consumption curves. Like the previous nomogram on weight-horsepower ratios, it allows for the tendency of manufacturers to overstate horsepower.

As an aside, most gas engines are rated with all power robbing accessories removed. They are wound up to maximum revolutions per minute (rpm) for very brief periods, and power output is measured before they blow apart. Obviously they deliver less horsepower in actual service.

Diesel engines are measured at service speeds, and the horsepower ratings are more accurate. Diesels, however, are extremely rare in small powerboats because of their very high weight-to-horse-

*Use this nomogram to compute fuel consumption. Because engine rpm's vary, write in full-throttle rpm opposite 100 percent throttle, for your engine. Then write down corresponding percentages. (If 5000 rpm is full-bore, 100 percent, then 2500 would be 50 percent, and so on.) Using a straightedge, connect percent of throttle on left with manufacturer's rated horsepower on right. Read probable fuel consumption where straightedge intersects center scale—two-cycle engines on left, four-cycles on right side of line.*

FUEL CONSUMPTION NOMOGRAM

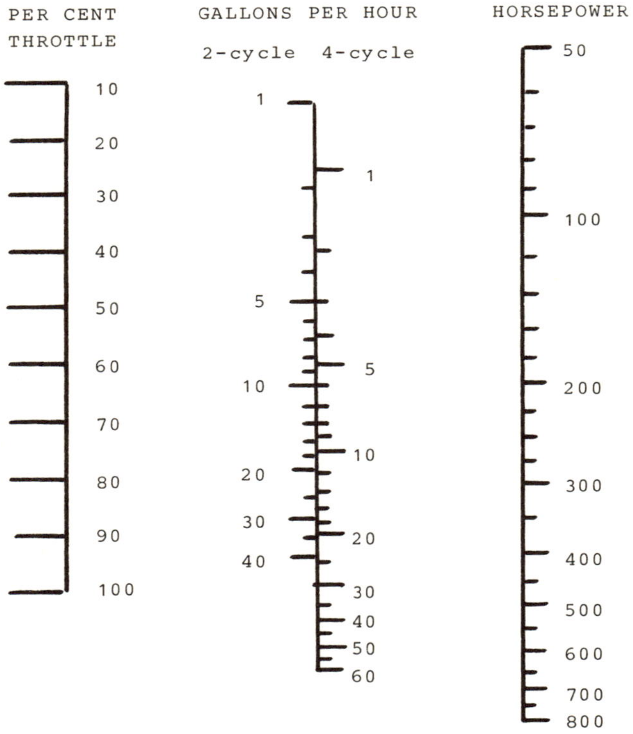

power ratios. They just aren't suitable for runabouts and smaller, lively craft.

Use the earlier nomogram to help select the power package for a boat. It will tell you what speed you can expect in service—don't forget that's a *top* speed figure. Then employ the fuel-consumption nomogram to find what kind of fuel consumption you can expect. It's in gallons per hour for good reason—that's the way the boating world figures it, because adverse winds, seas, and currents can enormously change any computation in miles per gallon. Boatmen prefer to use "cruising range" as a measure of consumption, since it is assumed weather and water conditions average out over the length of time it takes to use up a tankful of gas. They like to know how far they'll go on a tankful rather than a gallon.

However, miles per gallon is still useful as a tool for comparison. Take the top speed you expect, use the fuel-consumption nomogram, and you can figure how many miles you'll get to a gallon out of any boat-motor combination.

Then remember this rough rule: back off on the throttle by one-third, and you can reduce fuel consumption one-half. Speed does not drop proportionately. It may go down just 10 percent, rarely more than 20, depending on the hull-bottom lines.

You can come up with a pretty fair guess on probable fuel consumption. If you don't like the figures, take a look at another boat-motor combination.

# WHAT DO YOU ADD TO THE BOAT?

## The Coast Guard Package

You will definitely have to equip your boat with a certain amount of safety gear required by government regulations. Most dealers call it a "Coast Guard package." The most important item included in this package is the so-called personal flotation device, or PFD. The Coast Guard has a rather complex series of definitions by type, with specific details on the construction and degree of buoyancy. Basically, however, there are only two types: wearable devices and throwables. Life jackets and vests fall into the first category. Buoyant cushions, ring buoys, and horseshoe buoys are in the second. The type you must carry as a primary PFD depends on the size of your boat.

*Every boat must carry emergency gear, some required by law. These girls are completely equipped.*

Left: *Most powerboats must have a fire extinguisher. This one is larger than necessary for type of boat, but provides extra margin of safety.* Right: *Even dogs may need PFDs—and they make 'em!*

On boats under 16 feet in length, plus canoes and kayaks which may be longer, you must carry one buoyant cushion for each person on board. You do not need wearable PFDs, although the Coast Guard recommends them. Buoyant cushions have serious defects, but the Coast Guard realizes they are often the only practical PFD for really small craft.

If your boat is 16 feet or longer, you must have one wearable PFD for each person on board, plus one throwable device for use in man-overboard emergencies. The throwable device can be a ring buoy, which most people call a "life ring," a horseshoe buoy, or a buoyant cushion.

Wearable devices are superior, which is why they are required by law on slightly larger craft. The cushion is deceptive. It has straps on the sides, and people instinctively think they are supposed to be worn knapsack-style. This is extremely dangerous. If you wear a cushion like a knapsack, the buoyancy will be behind you. It will push you on your face. An exhausted swimmer can drown.

Various authorities suggest that you are supposed to put one leg through one strap, and the opposite arm through the other. The cushion then supports you in the water, riding on your chest. Unfortunately, most authorities never took a buoyant cushion into the water and tried it. It will work only for women and children. The straps are too small for most men. All you can really do with a buoyant cushion is clutch it to your chest and hang on—until you are too tired to hang on any longer, which is why the Coast Guard urges all skippers to equip their boats with wearable PFDs. When wearing a jacket or vest, you don't have to work to stay afloat.

It is therefore important to note that you can carry wearable PFDs on any boat, even canoes and kayaks and boats under 16 feet long. But if you choose buoyant cushions as primary PFDs, they are legal only on boats of the same class—you cannot depend on them for larger craft.

The law also requires you to keep your PFDs "readily available." You must remove them from their plastic wrappings. Do not leave them in those protective covers—that's the law. And do not stow them in out-of-the-way lockers. Keep them handy. The one throwable device required must always be in the cockpit, ready at hand for use in an emergency.

Now for a word about buying PFDs. The Coast Guard approves each manufacturer's product after examining samples. So you must buy only Coast Guard approved PFDs. They're so marked on the label. Do not make the error of buying a child's vest for an adult. They are a little cheaper, but check the label first.

Wearable PFDs have little plastic bags encasing the flotation material, and these are sewn into the vest or jacket. Occasionally—production lines being what they are—someone makes an error and a sewing machine needle pierces the plastic bag. You should gently squeeze a PFD in the store. If it slowly collapses under pressure, it has a pierced bag. Don't buy it.

Next on the list of legally required items is a fire extinguisher. Again, they are meticulously defined by type, but such details are unimportant to the small powerboat skipper. Just buy an approved dry chemical extinguisher. Why dry chemical? Because most fires on boats involve gasoline, and you can't quench such a blaze with water. The same dry chemical—a powder—works on electrical fires, where the use of water could be hazardous.

It's important to remember that the dry chemical in the ordinary fire extinguisher is a very fine powder, like talcum. It tends to pack down from the vibration of a boat; it can, in fact, cake into a hard mass. In such condition it might not work if you had to extinguish a tiny fire. To keep extinguishers in good condition, make it a habit to up-end the cylinder now and then, and pound on it with the heel of your hand to shake the powder loose—and keep it that way. Never use a hard tool, such as a hammer! You could rupture the extinguisher cylinder. Rap the thing with your hand every time you take the boat out, and the extinguisher will always work when you need it.

Never "test" an extinguisher by squeezing the trigger. The rest of the charge could leak away. Check the pressure gauge periodically. If you ever use the extinguisher, have it recharged immediately.

You do not have to carry an extinguisher if you own an outboard boat of completely open construction, with no enclosed bilges or other compartments in which fumes could accumulate. However, it's worth carrying anyway. I once saw a night fisherman knock over a gasoline lantern—which shouldn't be carried on boats in the first place. He got so panicky he tried to put out the fire by dipping water up in a fish landing net! A nearby skipper went to his aid with an extinguisher.

They can come in handy. For the record, you will probably never have a fire on an outboard. Statistically, only one out of every eighty thousand outboard boats has a fire each year. But carry an extinguisher in case it is your turn to become that number one.

Federal rules also require you to carry a whistle or horn if your boat is 16 feet or longer. It is required for signaling your intent in right-of-way situations. Admittedly, they are rarely used on smaller craft, but the law requires them.

And if your boat is 26 feet long or longer, you must have a bell. It'll come with the boat, in most cases. So will the required flame arrestor, in case you buy an inboard or sterndrive.

Some states have other requirements. Your dealer will know what they are. In any event, the Coast Guard at this writing is considering other requirements, which will probably become regulations in a short time. One is for a secondary means of propulsion. It can range from a spare kicker on the transom down to just an oar or paddle on smaller boats. The other is for what they refer to as a "de-watering" device, meaning a pump or bailer. These are common-sense items that belong on every boat, whether or not they are legally required.

You should also carry "distress" signals, a separate subject to be dealt with later. Distress is a dirty word evoking an image of sinking at sea, but in the vast majority of cases it may only be an engine malfunction. If you don't have that "secondary means of propulsion," you will need a tow home, and in many cases only a distress signal will attract attention to your plight. It's a fact that merely waving at other boats passing in the distance is usually misunderstood. The other people cheerily wave back and continue on their way. Flares or orange smoke signals bring the needed assistance.

## *What Extras Should You Buy?*

People who like boats really love gadgets. It's a rare skipper who doesn't add accessories. Some are almost essential, such as boarding ladders. Others, such as racks to hold your cold beverage, are only useful.

The most useful item you can add to your boat is a two-way radio. Again, the subject will be dealt with in more detail later. But for a few hundred dollars you have an invisible lifeline tied to the distant shore. Radiotelephones are almost a necessity in coastal areas, especially if you venture offshore.

Depth sounders or recorders are also useful accessories in big water. So are compasses, which become a must if you cruise the large bays and sounds along the coasts, or the Great Lakes.

Include a compass even if you never expect to see anything larger than a lake. When a blinding rainstorm strikes, they help you "keep your bearings" and can guide you back to the dock. All you have to do is aim your boat at the marina or dock and note the compass direction, just before the squall hits. It isn't "navigation." It's common sense to have a silent, magnetic guide back to the pier.

All boats should carry boarding ladders. Even for the young and agile, clambering back aboard from a swim can be strenuous work.

*This boat literally has everything, and shows how much you can add in the way of equipment: 1) Twin Outboards. 2) Lifting Eye. 3) Camper Top. 4) Downrigger (for deep trolling). 5) Running Light. 6) Folding Seat/Beds. 7) Folding Table. 8) Sounder/Locator. 9) VHF Marine Radio. 10) Horn. 11) Door to Cabin–2 Beds, Head, Storage Compartments. 12) Search Light. 13) CB Radio. 14) Cooler. 15) Sink & Water Supply. 16) Refrigerator. 17) Rod Holders. 18) Power Trim & Tilt. 19) Barometer. 20) Trim & Tilt Indicators. 21) Marine Clock. 22) Compass. 23) Engine Synchronizer. 24) Speedometer. 25) Tachometers. 26) Fuel Gauge.*

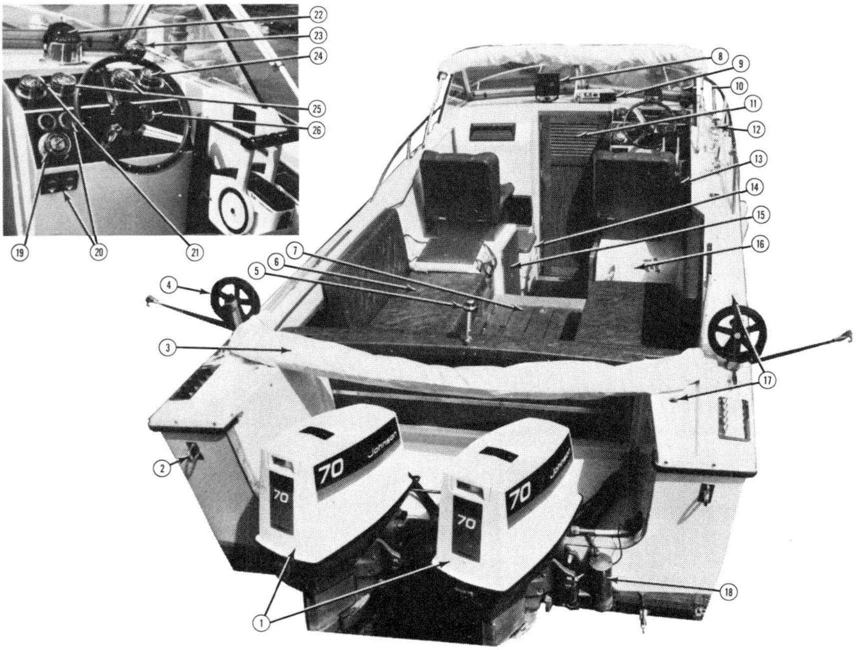

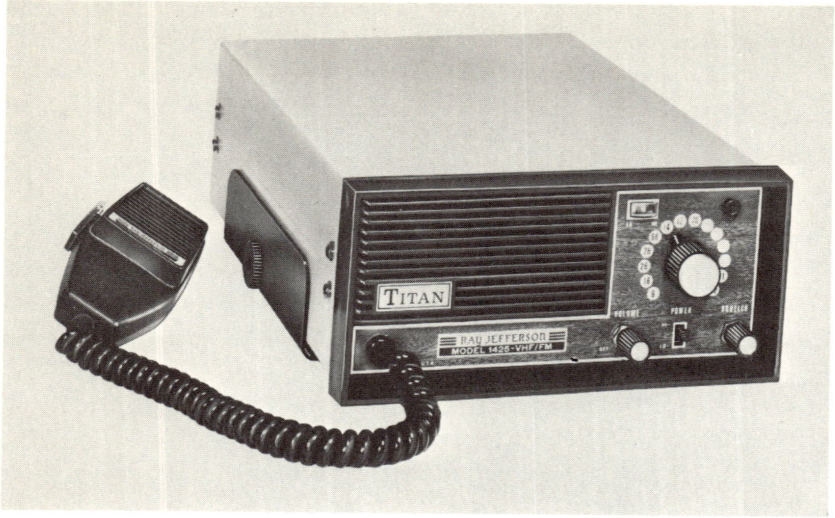


*Your first piece of optional equipment should be a two-way radio.*

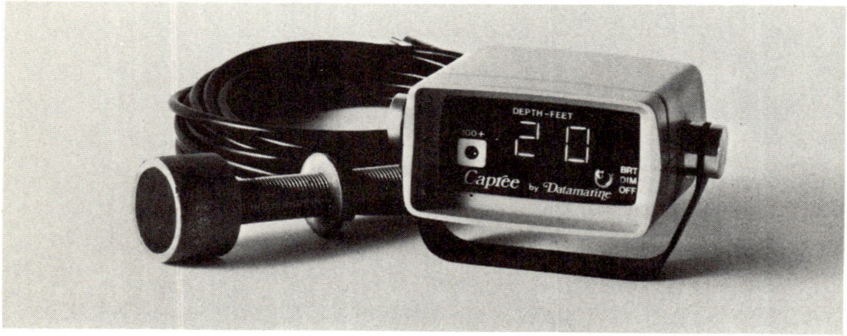


*This depth sounder reads directly in numerals, via a digital readout system.*

Hanging a ladder overside takes the sweat out of it, and for older people it's a necessity. You should also have properly made-up docklines, plus extra lengths of line for various and sundry uses. Anchors and anchor lines are a separate area to be treated in detail later.

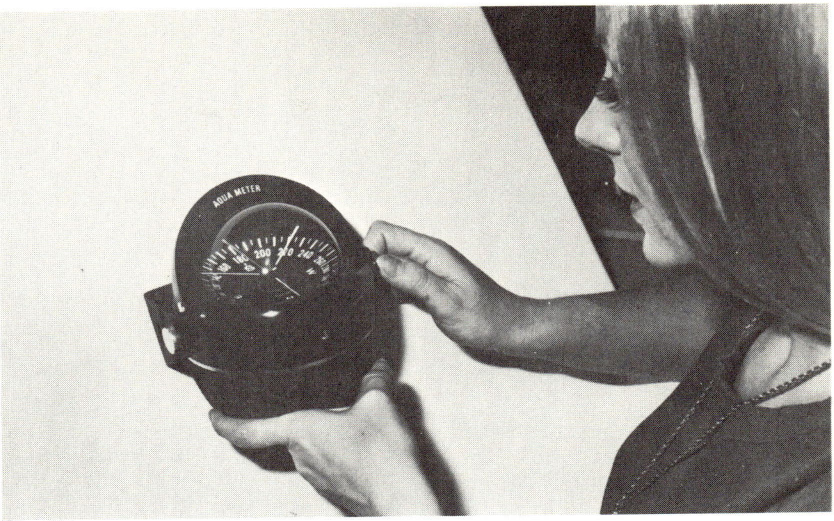


*Every boat should have a compass.*

Many people like to have a speedometer. They range in price from under $20 to three-figure sums, the latter varieties including an odometer that totals the miles traveled. Even the cheapies are surprisingly accurate, at least over a part of the speed range. And they can be adjusted.

These are the major items. Visit any marine store and you will find a truly astonishing number of accessories. Some, such as sea anchors, are valuable only to venturesome types who run far offshore. Others, such as anchor windlasses, save labor on heavy hulls. Without half-trying, you can run your accessory bill into four figures. Start out with only the necessary items; add the luxuries later.

## *For the Sake of Security*

Every powerboat skipper, for the most obvious of reasons, should carry basic tools and spare parts. No listing is necessary. You need wrenches, pliers, and screwdrivers to work on an engine. Spark

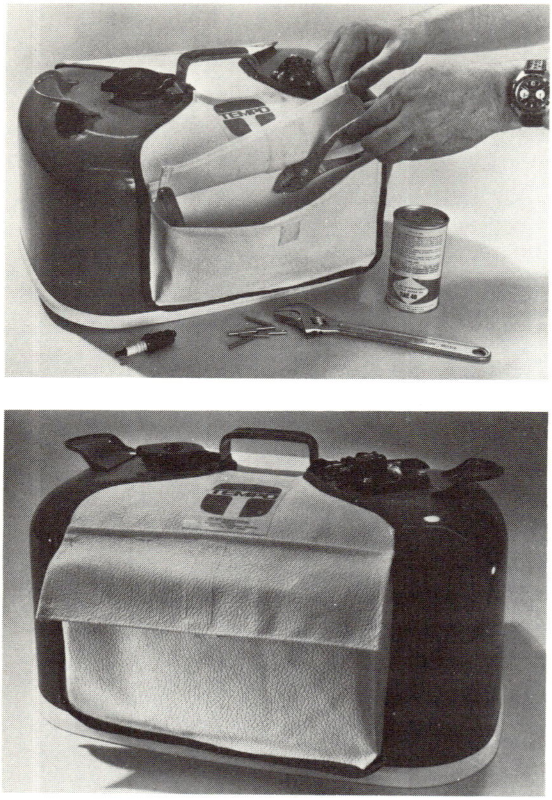

*Carry a basic tool kit. This one fits over standard portable outboard fuel tank.*

plugs are a must since fouled plugs cause more engine failures in outboards than perhaps any other factor. It's astonishing how often a misfiring, balky kicker revives when you replace the plugs.

Spare propellers are desirable, plus assorted propeller hardware, depending on the type of engine you have. Changing a propeller is child's play, but you get a sick feeling when a pin or other vital part falls into the water and sinks to the bottom.

Oddly enough a "junk box" is something that belongs on every boat. It carries a miscellany of odd lengths of wire, tape, extra fuses, lugs, nuts, bolts, washers, and the like. The more junk the better.

The greatest appeal of boating is its sense of freedom and independence. But to twist an old quote, the price of this liberty is eternal vigilance. It is downright shameful to beg for a tow home when a well-filled junk box and a couple of hand tools might have eliminated the problem.

Last, but not least, is a first-aid kit. You can buy one at any marine dealer. Since it will contain only the bare essentials for treating cuts and scratches, you might consider adding a few extras, such as aspirin, indigestion remedies, sunburn lotions, and even seasickness pills for friends with tender tummies.

When you do get your boat equipped, seek out the nearest Coast Guard Auxiliary and request a Courtesy Motorboat Examination. The CME decal is of value in itself, but knowing you are properly equipped is most important of all.

# SELECTING WHEELS FOR THE KEEL

## *The Towing Vehicle*

Some boat buyers should really look at the family auto or station wagon before they buy a powerboat. A small, foreign car with a tiny, four-cylinder engine may not have the muscle it takes to haul a boat on a trailer.

It depends on the combination, of course. This writer once towed a 16-foot boat with a tiny English roadster, and never had a single problem. It is smart, however, to check with your auto dealer and inquire about your particular car. He can suggest safe limits. Maybe he can add useful accessories, like load levelers. New autos, if you are in the market for one, can be equipped with towing packages. Whichever route you take, just be sure you can handle the trailer weight. If you can't, you'll pay the price in overheating engines and excessive wear and tear. Luckily, most American cars—including six-cylinder compacts—can handle the average, reasonably light boat.

*The towing vehicle is as important as the boat.*

## Selecting a Trailer

In choosing a trailer, be certain to check its load capacity. Some dealers keep package prices low by putting cheapie trailers under their hulls. Satisfy yourself that the trailer will hold your load. Include in your calculations not only the weight of boat and engine, but the gasoline—at six pounds per gallon—and other extras you will add. Make a decent extra allowance for the sake of safety.

Avoid at all costs those really tiny trailer tires, even if you tow a very light boat. When your auto's doing a nice, safe, legal 50 miles per hour the ultrasmall trailer wheels are turning at the equivalent of 80 or more. This is hard on the bearings.

Ideally, the wheels and tires of your trailer should match those on your car, in which case your auto spare also serves the trailer.

*This spare trailer tire doubles in brass as a dolly when moving the trailer around.*

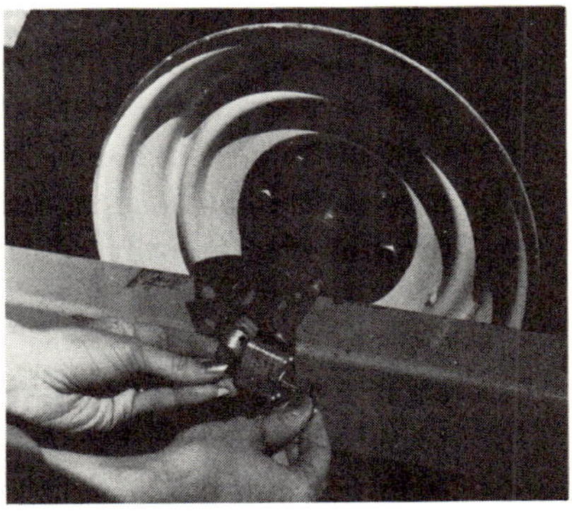

Also, such standard sizes can be bought at almost every gas station while smaller trailer tires cannot.

When an odd-sized trailer tire goes flat on a Saturday morning, it can ruin your entire weekend. For this reason, if you can't match your auto tires, buy a spare trailer wheel and tire. It can be bolted to the trailer frame. Get a jack designed for trailers, too. Your regular auto bumper jack, a Detroit abomination, could be useless.

Be sure the trailer adequately supports the bottom of the boat—down the length of the keel, and under the sides. It's especially important to have good support across the transom, and the boat's stern should not hang far over the rear of the trailer.

Launching problems related to boat size and weight have brought about the development of different trailer types. The simplest, for light hulls, is just a common bed trailer. You shove the boat off—period. For somewhat heavier boats there's a break-frame trailer. Unlock it at the forward end, and the bed tilts up. It's easier to slide a boat off, or winch it back on. At the top of the line you have trailers designed to go into the water, so you can literally float the boat on or off. Vertical posts on the sides keep the hull properly aligned; and the necessary trailer lights are mounted atop the rear posts so the wiring isn't submerged. With such a trailer—and a proper towing vehicle—you can handle astonishingly large craft, as long as they are within the eight-foot maximum beam permitted on the highways.

## *Hitching up the Trailer*

The question of hitches is an important one. Never, never, trust a simple bumper hitch when towing a boat, even a small one. They may be fine for rental trailers when you want to take some trash to the county dump, but they lack the security for regular use.

Start out with a frame hitch, which your auto dealer may be able to install. It is far more secure. And anytime the total weight of boat and trailer approaches 2,000 pounds, consider a weight equalization hitch, which better distributes the load on the rear of the towing vehicle. They cost more, to be sure, but you won't create a spectacle by driving down the highway looking as if you were trying to climb a

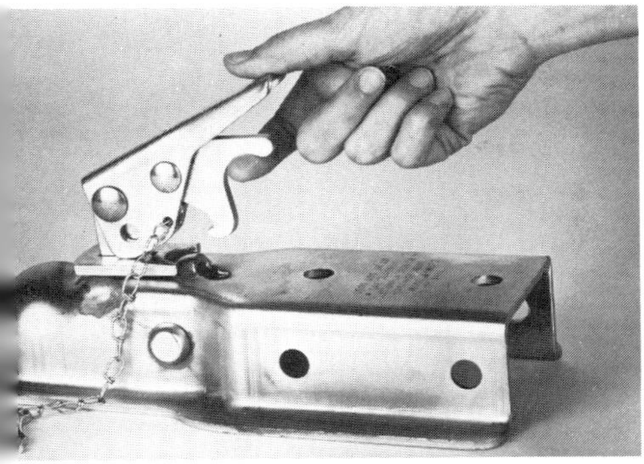

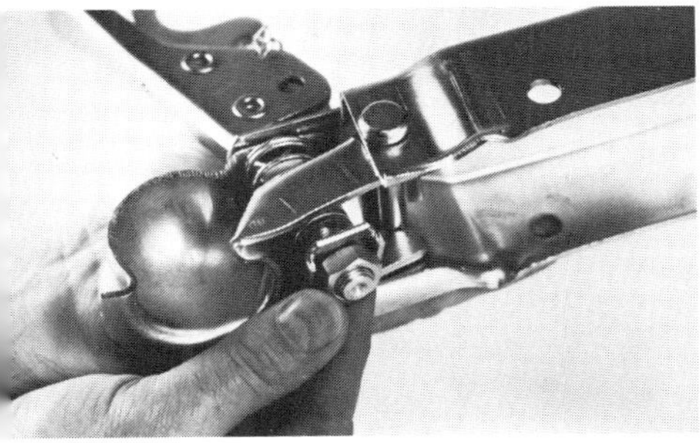

*A simple hand winch is adequate for smaller boats.*

*A safe, sturdy hitch is essential.*

hill, with the auto's rear end sagging and the front pointing skyward. Not only is it silly, and hard on the car, but it probably puts you in violation of the law. Your headlights are now aimed upward into the eyes of oncoming motorists, rather than straight down the road where they belong.

Your dealer will know what lights and reflectors your rig will require. You'll have to have turn signals, stop lights, and license illumination. They plug into your auto system, and the wiring job is a simple one. Because of the increased electrical load, a heavy-duty flasher must be substituted for the standard unit in your auto. It's a 60-second chore, and a cheap one.

Safety chains are a must. Trailer tongues lock on a ball that is part of the hitch. It can be one and seven-eighths inches for small boats, should be two inches in diameter for larger ones. Pick the larger ball anyway. It's better. Balls do wear out of round, however, and should be replaced if this is suspected. And trailers do sometimes separate from the towing vehicle. Hence the safety chain. Don't allow any more slack than you need for turns. It should be short enough to hold the trailer tongue off the road if it separates.

Start thinking about trailer brakes when the total load reaches 1,500 pounds, and add them for sure if it hits 2,000. They can be electrical, or surge-hydraulic, the latter operating independently through inertia. Either way, they should be rigged to operate if the trailer comes loose. Check your state laws, but they may be conservative. Brakes can be important on heavier trailer rigs.

Winches are necessary, and should have the power to handle the boat. You can crank yourself into a coronary with a tiny winch not

*Electric power winches take all the work out of cranking.*

*Be sure you have some form of adequate tie-down to secure your boat on the trailer.*

geared to the load. Electric winches are a luxury, but if you've ever tried one you'd call them necessities. They take all the work out of reloading a boat, and are a must on hulls approaching a ton in weight—unless you are built like an ape and don't get winded easily. Again, check the capacity. Weak winches break down; those with adequate power do not. As a safety measure, few dealers are anxious to face the risks of liability suits by peddling inferior and inadequate winches, cables, and hooks, so it isn't a serious problem.

Don't forget that you'll probably need special towing mirrors, sticking out far enough from the car so you have a clear view to the rear. They are detachable, of course, when the boat is not being towed, and are not particularly costly.

A few final words on trailers: bearing troubles seem to be the only common trailer problem. They obviously are minimized or eliminated if you just get into the habit of having your bearings checked regularly and repacked with a proper grease. You can buy special types of bearings and seals that ease the chore of keeping them full of grease. Ask your dealer about them. Whatever you do, however, try to avoid submerging the bearings when launching a boat. They heat up on the highway, and when dunked in cool water they create a vacuum which can draw in dirt and gunk and water and trouble.

Be sure you add tie-down straps. They hold a boat on a trailer. People have towed boats without them, and the boats have sometimes flipped off the trailers when they hit a hard turn. Secure the boat well.

Also, pick up a special tire gauge if you have regular trailer tires rather than auto types. Trailer tires, as a rule, take more than the 50 pounds of pressure, which is the top reading on the average gas station gauge. You'll find high pressure gauges at auto supply stores. They aren't expensive—and you'll need one.

## PAPERWORK AND RED TAPE

In all but a few states there are registration laws. Boats must be issued numbers, just like autos. Some states also have title laws, designed to impede thievery and illegal sales. There may also be taxes in addition to registration fees. You'll learn all you care to know about this subject when you buy a boat, and it doesn't have to be spelled out here.

The real reason for bringing the subject up is to warn readers of these factors:

1. Whenever you buy a used boat, be sure the registration (and title, if your state has such a law) is transferred to your name. Buyers who overlook this detail run into massive red tape when the next state registration period rolls around and it's time to renew. As far as the state is concerned, you don't legally own that boat, and you'll have to go back and find the man who sold it to you, and hope his wife didn't toss the documents in the trash can.

2. Be very wary of bargain-priced boats, especially if they carry out-of-state registrations and are offered by individuals who seem anxious to unload them. There really is a lot of boat theft, and in some states police have broken up organized rings of pirates. If you

buy a stolen boat, and it is subsequently recovered by the owner, you may be out a lot of money. It has been known to happen.

Concluding the paperwork side of boat ownership, you'll probably have to finance your purchase. It's no different from buying a car "on time." Banks offer the best interest rates, but usually require a substantial down payment. Because of high interest rates, you're better off plunking a load of cash down on a boat.

And by all means, insure the boat. Insurance rates can be reasonable, sometimes as low as four percent of the value annually. I pay $250 per year on a boat valued at $6,000, and it includes a medical cost clause and a fat liability protection.

## CAN YOU WATER-TEST THE BOAT?

This part was left until last, because it is really the last thing to do when trying to make up your mind about a boat. Some dealers never provide water demonstrations, perhaps because they aren't close to a body of water. Others are willing to show off their product.

If you go out with a salesman on a water test, he will make it a point to show you how smoothly the boat can perform in bumpy going, even if he has to cross a cruiser wake to prove it. You can judge the softness of the ride, and the dryness—lack of spray—with someone else at the wheel. But these things you should do for yourself:

1. Note the acceleration, and bear in mind that a demonstrator is usually loaded lightly. Any good outboard or sterndrive should be up on plane and running easily in five seconds. Six or seven is tops even for the weekenders and cuddy cabin craft. Getting up on plane sluggishly is a sign of inadequate power.

2. Boats should turn easily, in both directions, without excessive banking. Never, never, wind a strange boat up to full speed and then put the helm hard over. This stunt is for professional boat testers, and even they don't do it without working up to it slowly.

Put the helm in a hard turn, at slow speed, and ease the throttle up slowly but not all the way. If the boat has a tendency to skid out at the stern, or produce propeller "ventilation" in which the prop loses its bite and races, it'll show up here.

3. There should be no steering torque, which is to say the boat shouldn't pull one way or the other, at any speed. Sometimes you'll have a trace of torque as you accelerate, and it vanishes at cruising speed. This is acceptable. The torque, or turning force, produced by the propellers was adjusted for elimination at the boat's intended cruising speed.

In severe cases, the boat will pull hard to one side, and turns made in that direction are difficult to pull out of until you slow down almost to a halt. This is poor performance.

You also want to check the lateral stability by moving from one side to the other. You don't want a boat that is tender, although some degree of it will have to go with any deep-vee hull designed for high performance, especially in smaller lengths.

If you can do so, time the boat on a measured distance and compute its top speed. Compare this with the nomogram on weight-horsepower ratios. If a boat can't move at a top speed within 85 to 90 percent of those you compute from the nomogram and the weight-horsepower ratio, you have an inefficient bottom design, an engine not putting out all its rated power, or other problems. Avoid it.

*PART TWO*

# *Maintaining a Powerboat*

# *KEEPING EVERYTHING SHIPSHAPE*

## *Begin with the First Trip*

Maintenance starts the minute you take your boat out for the first time. Neglect is expensive. So establish sound maintenance habits from the very beginning. You'll save money, prevent trouble from developing, maintain a higher trade-in value, and enjoy boating more.

As soon as you can, after hauling the boat out of the water, hose the hull down thoroughly with fresh water. Clean and wipe down all the hardware. Use a demoisturant spray (there are several makes on the market) on rails, cleats, and other hardware items.

Engines also need attention on every trip. Note has already been made of idling down four-cycle engines before shutting them down. Outboards have their little quirks, too.

If you expect it will be some time before you use your boat again, disconnect the fuel line on an outboard and let all the gas in the carburetor burn out. It will prevent the formation of gum, which can lead to hard starting later. This isn't important if you use your boat two or three times a month, but clear the carb if you know you won't be using the boat for three weeks or a month.

If you have a boat with a large main engine and a spare emergency kicker on a retractable transom mount, get in the habit of using that spare engine briefly at the end of every trip or so. Even if you just lower it in the water and let it idle in dock, do so. Retractable

*Check propeller for nicks or damage when you haul the boat.*

mounts, long unused, can freeze up. Engines need exercise too, now and then. And you want that spare to function in case of need, so don't neglect it.

Any time you haul a boat out of the water, check the propeller for nicks and other possible damage. See if any monofilament line has gotten wrapped around the shaft. It has happened to a few people who fish, experience backlashes or tangled line, cut it away and toss it overboard. It can tangle in a prop, which wraps it around the shaft. Occasionally the shaft seal has been broken by the line. So look for lower unit damage or other problems.

And this rule should be followed on every single trip: top off your fuel tanks before you take the boat home. The reason is that atmospheric moisture can condense inside a half-filled tank. It means a slow accumulation of water in the gasoline and an ultimate stoppage. Keeping the tanks filled with gas all but eliminates this problem. So top them off at the end of each boating day.

## *What to Do at Home*

When you get the boat home and unhitch it, raise the tongue. You may have a large boat, and use a combination dolly and jack—very handy. Or you may use just a stand. Whatever the means, tilt the boat so the bow is slightly raised. You want rainwater to drain out.

If you didn't already pull the transom drain at the ramp, remove it now so no water can accumulate in the boat. And here's an unusual tip, if you live in an area plagued by mosquitoes. Most boats have a

*Covering a boat can encourage mildew, especially in warmer and humid climates.*

"sump" at the transom, and they will always hold a little water—in which mosquitoes can breed. So stick a strip of toweling in through the drain so it serves as a wick to keep the sump drained. It's a minor item, but in a town loaded with trailerboats all those sumps can breed a respectable brood of pesky bugs.

Avoid covering a boat if you can, and never, never cover an outboard engine. It encourages dampness and humidity, which can raise hob with the ignition system. The best weather protection for a trailerboat is a carport or garage, which poses obvious problems. If you can afford it, the next best bet is a portable-type carport, a frame with canvas top. Check your zoning laws in any event. There may be special restrictions on storing boats, such as a size limit—no problem to most people—or a requirement that a boat be kept to the rear of the house line.

This is as good a time as any to digress and mention the dry-storage marinas in major boating areas. These "in-and-out" facilities keep your boat on a rack, using a fork lift truck to put it in the water.

They're very convenient, spare you much trouble since the usual procedure is to hose the boat down for you, top the tanks, and keep it ready to go on call. When the racks are in a sturdy shed, you have perfect weather protection even from storms. Costs are within reason, and you do save the price of a trailer. But you will sacrifice a certain mobility. You start all your voyages from the same dock. With a trailer you can haul a boat hundreds of miles on a weekend and explore distant areas.

Marinas are worth considering, however. They're quite popular in south Florida (where they originated) because they are built to withstand hurricane-force winds, so a boatowner can forget about storm problems.

## *What About Theft?*

You might as well face the fact that boats do attract thieves, although in most suburban areas it's no great problem. So take your valuables inside. Even radios can be installed with special mounts so the unit can be slipped out and stored in the house.

By all means consider a burglar alarm system. A whole book could be written on this subject alone, but check your marine dealer and auto supply store for information. Probably the cheapest and best system you can install on a trailerboat is any burglar alarm utilizing a "pendulum switch." It's sensitive to movement. If a thief jogs your trailer, as he would have to, whether trying to hoist off the outboard engine or hitch up the whole rig, it can set off a piercing alarm. Experts claim that nothing shatters a burglar's already taut nerves like a loud noise. Even if you aren't home, the odds are burglars will flee and leave your boat behind if it has such an alarm system.

Cost is quite low. The switch, heart of the system, shouldn't come to much more than $10 or so and you can install a complete alarm yourself. Be sure to wire in a cut-off switch and remember to use it when you hitch up the boat yourself, or you'll wake up the whole neighborhood to witness your red-faced, pre-dawn departure on a fishing trip.

## *Taking Care of the Engine*

If you use your boat in salt water, flush out the cooling system at regular intervals. Flushing attachments are sold for outboards and sterndrives. They're simple to use, permit hooking up a garden hose and cleaning out the cooling system with fresh water. It's wise to use them now and then, even if you're an inland boatman. Buy the right kind, and read the directions. Never run up the engine to high rpm. Just let it idle.

Americans are notorious for trusting their mechanical instincts, sometimes to their sorrow, hence the sardonic quip, "When all else fails, read the directions." Always read your motor manual! Pay particular attention to the directions on checking the motor's lower unit for lubrication. It varies from one make to another, but generally there's one plug for filling and one for draining. Use the right lubricant. Remove the drain plug now and then, and if a watery, milky fluid runs out, drain and refill immediately—and check the oil seal on the drive shaft.

Sterndrives may have an upper gearcase fill, with an intercon-

Left: *Flush out engine with fresh water at regular intervals.*
Right: *Check lower unit gear case for grease, and keep it lubricated, no matter how messy you may think it is!*

necting gallery leading to the lower unit, so you can easily add lubrication. Check your owner's manual, as suggested. Lack of oil can mean a costly repair job. Don't neglect this chore.

An outboarder's best friend is grease—and it helps any boatman. Every now and then grease everything on the boat and engine that is supposed to move. This includes all control linkages, steering, tilt mechanisms. Several good brands of general-purpose grease are sold. Keep one handy, and be generous with it. Neglect can mean frozen controls, hard steering, and on those retractable transom mounts for spare engines, a stuck and frozen mount that won't lower the engine into the water. Follow this simple rule: grease everything that moves, or is supposed to, or is an adjustment—like the steering tension adjustment on outboard engines. Grease is cheap. So don't be afraid to waste a little.

Make it a point to go over your fuel system from time to time. It's not so important on an outboard with portable fuel tanks—a simple glance will suffice to tell you whether the flexible lines are still in good condition, without cracks developing. Those lines can wear, of course, and often it's at the engine end which seems to take the most flexing. If a crack develops, you can simply remove the clamp, cut off a few inches of hose, and replace the fitting. On permanently installed systems, it pays to periodically check everything from the deck fill fittings to the lines, the tank, and valves if any.

Remember the earlier warning that modern fiberglass boats will outlast their fuel systems. Be more diligent as time passes. Ultimately

*Pull the prop and clean the shaft several times each season.*

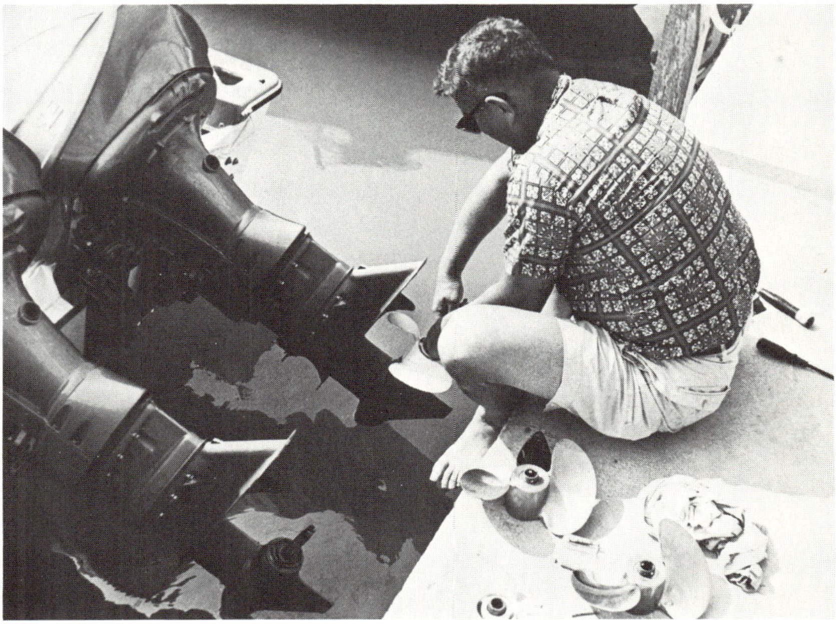

you may have to replace something, whether it's a simple item like a hose clamp or something more complicated, like the tank itself.

You'll also postpone problems if you'll regularly examine the spark plugs, and install a new set when they seem badly fouled. It's a personal thing with this writer, but I have found that it's easier to replace plugs than to try to clean badly fouled ones. Most of us don't have high-pressure air hoses, although you could always trot your blackened plugs down to the friendly gas station owner on the corner and borrow his.

There's one very important item of periodic, preventive maintenance that you simply must not overlook. Make it a point to remove

*This is what can happen to a lower unit left in the water too long.*

your propeller every now and then. If you don't, it can freeze in place on the shaft! Probably no single other factor can prove so aggravating to the novice boatman. Neglect this chore, and someday you may have to remove a prop—perhaps because of damage. So pull the prop every now and again. Clean the shaft thoroughly—a strip of sandpaper helps immensely. Get all the crud off the shaft.

Then grease it thoroughly—there's your best friend at work for you again. Smear on all-purpose grease or, if your dealer has it, a grease recommended for the purpose, and replace the propeller.

Frozen props are all but impossible to get off. You can locate a block of wood on a strategic spot, and rap it with a hammer (the wood protects the propeller) but it doesn't always work. You can perhaps adapt a gear-puller if you have one. You can buy a special propeller puller—which is expensive; or you can tow the rig down to the dealer's where an employee will perhaps use a pneumatic gadget to knock it off. Better that you do it yourself at regular intervals, so you won't get in such a bind.

One final item you should inspect at somewhat longer intervals: your steering trim tabs. They are tiny, rudder-like appendages on the lower units of outboards or sterndrives, sticking down into the discharge cone area behind the propeller.

They have two purposes, one of which is to correct for torque in the steering. Mention was made of this earlier. Propellers tend to develop unequal thrust. A trim tab can be set at an angle to neutralize the inequality.

The tabs are usually made of zinc, and are not painted for good reason: they double as anti-corrosion gadgets. This calls for a brief digression. When you immerse two dissimilar metals in water (which serves as an electrolyte), you create a battery. A weak electric current will flow from the less noble metal, which is the anode of the battery. Aluminum is anodic to steel and other higher metals on the galvanic scale, and lower unit housings are aluminum while drive shafts and other parts of the engine are steel.

So the aluminum will slowly erode in this natural, galvanic process. Zinc is lower on the galvanic scale than even aluminum, so they make the trim tabs out of zinc. They are not painted because paint would prevent them from doing their duty, which is to sacrifice themselves to protect the aluminum. So, trim tabs do wear away slowly. You may notice it first as torque develops in previously torque-free steering.

However, it pays to check the tabs as the engine ages. In time, they will obviously require replacement. They're cheap, and you can do the job yourself. But put the new ones back at exactly the same angle as the ones you remove! Otherwise, you'll have poor steering, pulling to one side.

Trim tabs are adjusted easily if you keep this crazy fact in mind: Set them to steer *toward* the side where you experience the pull of torque. In other words, if the boat pulls to port (left), set the tab, as if it were a rudder, so it will turn the boat to port. It'll correct the pull. Why? Because the tab steers the engine, not the boat. Angle it to the left, and it actually tends to push the engine *to the right*, which corrects the torque effect. It takes a little thinking, but becomes clear, especially if you go look at the outboard lower unit and consider the effect of the tab.

In any event, tabs do wear out—faster when a boat is used heavily in salt water. So glance at them now and again to check their condition.

## Keep the Boat Clean

Modern fiberglass hulls (or aluminum, for that matter) need little attention. But the hulls, just like automobiles, keep their good looks longer if they are cleaned and waxed occasionally.

Fiberglass has a tendency to develop chalkiness, and waxing slows down this surface effect. It's hard work, considerably eased if you have power buffers to help, and most people do have some form of home drill or sander to which a buffing pad can be attached.

It's my own feeling that nothing is as good as a paste wax, well rubbed in, but opinions on this will differ. Take your choice of cleaners and various waxes, but use them. Needless to say, it adds much to the resale or trade-in value of the boat.

It pays to go over the convertible top and camping or mooring covers now and then. Mildew may be forming, and a suitable cleaner will combat it. A little clear grease, such as Vaseline, helps keep glove snaps clean and free from crud and corrosion. It's irritating to try and snap on a camping cover you haven't used for some time and find the snaps so fouled they don't work. Try a petroleum jelly. It works.

Go over the hardware, too. Cheap cleats and rails start flaking early on, which is why it pays to buy a boat with good hardware. In any event, keep them clean, wipe them down with a little light grease on your hand, or a special rust-preventive that will delay corrosion. Check the bolts or fastenings on rails and cleats. They hardly ever vibrate loose on a good boat, but on a cheapie it pays to check.

*Keep hardware clean, using special sprays or even light grease for protection.*

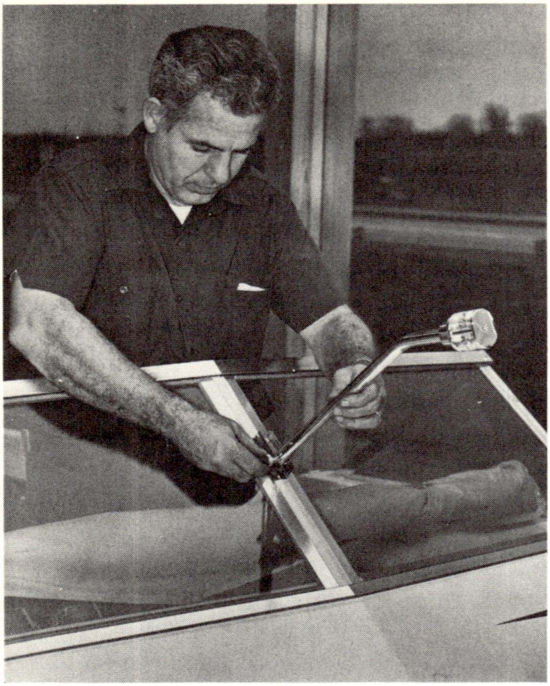

*Disassemble navigation lights and clean them thoroughly at least once a year.*

## Navigation Lights

A special note is advisable on your navigation lights, which are required by law on any boat operated at night. As an aside, Uncle Sam won't insist you have them, as long as you don't use your boat after dark, but some states require them on the grounds that you may be caught out unexpectedly after sunset. Most boats come with such lights installed.

You should take your lights apart at least once a year, and it wouldn't hurt to double that in coastal waters. Do so for the same reason you pull the prop now and then. The globe assemblies, even the bulbs, can freeze in place, locked in by rust or corrosion. Keep them clean.

When you buy a new boat, it pays to take the lights apart and smear a little light grease, like Vaseline, on all threaded parts, assembly points, and even the socket and bulb. There are other products that can also serve, some in spray cans.

A thin film of light grease does not break the circuit. The lights will still work, and they will be protected, to a certain degree, against corrosion.

This kind of regular attention prevents problems when a bulb burns out. The powerboat skipper who is unaware of these minor preventive maintenance steps learns the hard way—when he tries to change a bulb.

## *The Trailer*

Trailers, particularly those that resist rusting, are pretty durable beasts of burden. But look them over from time to time. Sand down and paint rust specks when they appear. You can also buy galvanize in a spray can.

Obviously you should check the bearings from time to time. It's no joke to have them burn out on the road. As noted in the earlier section on buying trailers, you can equip them with special devices that virtually ensure adequate lubrication.

Tires also should be examined for nicks and cuts. Tread wear usually is no problem on the average rig.

Check the winch and cable from time to time. Take no chances on a cable that shows signs of fraying or excessive wear. It's potentially dangerous. Should it snap under strain while hauling a boat out, it could lash out like a whip and injure someone. Replace any worn cable.

It also pays to keep an eye on the trailer wiring and lights. Obviously bulbs burn out, which is why it was suggested earlier you check the lights each time you hitch up the auto. The alternative is a citation from a highway patrolman.

A total novice may by this time have gotten the feeling that owning a boat is more trouble than it is worth. Well, even golfers will scrub a ball on the course, and clean their clubs from time to time.

Tennis players may have to have a racket restrung. All sports equipment requires care.

A boat is probably the third most costly item you can buy, after a home and a car. And it is infinitely more complex than a set of golf clubs. Hence it calls for more care.

It pays to establish good *preventive* maintenance habits with your very first trip. The items outlined in this section take but a few minutes each, and are spread out over months. The neophyte mariner who knows nothing about them inevitably must agonize over painful repair and replacement chores. But the boating beginner who starts out with some idea of what he should do to keep everything shipshape will rarely have any trouble with his boat, engine, and trailer.

# *ENSURING EFFICIENT PERFORMANCE*

## *Solving Hull Problems*

In the section on buying a boat, warning was given that people have a tendency to add a lot of equipment and gear to a boat. Now is the time to point out that you must distribute the load as evenly as possible.

The smaller the boat, the more important it is. But it can happen on any hull. A major builder of yachts in this country tests every model exhaustively, and publishes in its advertisements (as many builders do) the probable speed and other performance figures.

When a buyer contacts the factory to complain that his $80,000 purchase isn't coming up to snuff the factory experts drag out their books and ask, almost wearily, "Okay, what did you buy and where did you install it?"

It is very easy to upset the design trim of a boat—any boat. A few builders are so aware of this fact they even install fuel tanks so the trim of the boat will not change as the fuel is consumed. This calls for delicate planning, and you won't find it on many smaller boats, especially outboards.

To avoid running bow-down, or with the stern squatting, stow your weighty gear with some thought. Try to distribute the load evenly, and don't put too much aboard anyway.

I've known highly skilled fishermen who bought 16- or 18-foot craft, then added extra fuel capacity, up to 50 gallons (at six pounds per gallon), huge ice chests, sometimes custom-built to take 100 or more pounds of ice, plus other equipment, and located everything at the stern of the boat because it was handy, and left the bow area clear for casting. Then they wondered why the boat squatted, struggled to climb on plane, plowed sluggishly, and never reached its optimum speed.

It is extremely important not to overload a boat, and not to load it unevenly. Sometimes it can't be helped. Sometimes you induce squat, and know it, but have no choice because you want that extra fuel capacity or whatever.

There are two things you can do to help: First, consider adding trim tabs. These gadgets are like the elevators on an airplane. They are installed at the transom bottom, extending aft, and can be adjusted to angle slightly downward. The effect is to produce lift at the stern, as the water is deflected by the tabs. Trim tabs can work marvelous cures on even stubborn cases of squat. They produce significant savings of fuel in doing so, since the boat is no longer trying to climb out of a hole in the water. It can level off and run the way it was meant to run.

Trim tabs can cost less than $20 for a small powerboat. They are easy to install, and are adjusted manually, locking in place. You can set them by guesstimate, try the boat, and adjust again until you have them set right for your average load.

The disadvantage is that you can't change the adjustment while running. You have to stop the boat, and changing the tab angle isn't easy when the boat's afloat. For this reason—and because poor trim is a problem on many, many boats—enterprising manufacturers offer a variety of trim tabs with electric and hydraulic power adjustment ability. Costs can rise to $400, but that's for a fairly large boat. Adjustable trim tabs allow you to keep the boat in proper running trim at all times, changing it to suit the load and the water conditions.

On most boats, regardless of design, the ride will be smoother in rough water if you can trim the boat slightly down by the bow. It is

*Boat in bottom photo is squatting, running bow high, due to poorly distributed load. With trim tabs added, it has proper running trim (top photo).*

helpful, when running before a sea, to change the trim so the boat is slightly down by the stern, with the bow higher. (The difference is only a few degrees, and not apparent to the unskilled eye, but it makes a whale of a difference in performance.)

Adjustable power trim units on outboards and sterndrives help, but when you also have load problems, only adjustable trim tabs meet the issue squarely and keep you on that even keel. Good running trim is essential to efficient performance, and highly desirable in these days when gasoline isn't cheap.

It should go without saying that you must keep the bottom clean—and it helps if it is waxed occasionally. Never permit fouling growth to accumulate. The speed loss is monstrous. In coastal areas, and admittedly on boats normally kept afloat with protective anti-fouling paint, the growth of barnacles and "grass," or algae, can be relatively swift. Often it may reach a point where a powerboat won't

*Trim tabs are installed on the boat transom, and are easily adjusted.*

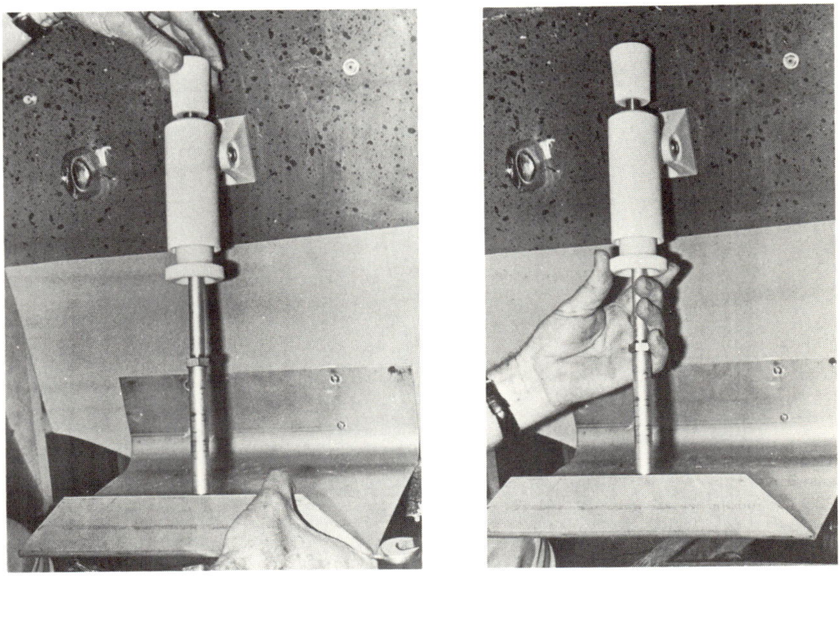

plane. Long before then fuel waste can reach 25 percent. Where you once burned four gallons, you can burn five. So keep the bottom clean—no problem on a trailerboat. The slicker it is, the better, so consider waxing the bottom now and then.

## *An Efficient Engine*

Any engine performs best when it is tuned to the manufacturer's specifications. If you have any doubts, they may be resolved by a brief report on the results of some tests conducted by a major firm in the marine power field.

They borrowed 14 boats, mostly sterndrives with some inboards but no outboards, from their owners. They wanted typical powerboats, well used by average boatmen.

First, they found evidence of woeful routine maintenance. Every single carburetor was out of whack and required adjustment; many had to be cleaned; several even had to be rebuilt. On quite a few boats they also had to clean or even replace the fuel filters. And on all but one, they had to clean the flame arrestors. (Backfire flame arrestors are required by federal law on all inboard gasoline engines. They take the place of the air cleaner element on your auto engine. They should be routinely cleaned as part of any service shop tune-up, but the owner should "remind" the dealer when he delivers the boat.)

All the boats had been tested prior to tune-up, and were tested again afterward—with delicate instrumentation measuring fuel flow in thousandths of a gallon.

What did they find?

Fuel savings up to 17 percent after a tune-up. This was the highest figure of the 14 boats, but the average wasn't much lower. They also checked out what many experienced boatmen have known by instinct for years: that if you hold the boat speed down, you will save a lot of fuel.

Anyone knows, if he has any experience, that you can cut fuel use roughly in half, in terms of gallons per hour (gph) when you cut the throttle by one-third. Yet speed doesn't drop in the same ratio, so you gain in terms of miles per gallon (mpg). The test engineers found

*Even high-performance boats burn less fuel at cruising speed, need less engine maintenance.*

that maintaining a low cruise speed, rather than a high cruise (you find both by a seat-of-the-pants feel) significantly increased efficiency and fuel savings.

Adding it all up with their little pocket computers, they found that with a combination of a finely tuned engine, and a moderate cruise speed, you can reasonably expect a 25 percent improvement in performance and fuel consumption. Run a poorly tuned engine wide open, and you will pour away one gallon out of every four you buy.

Obviously, then, you should watch the engine and keep it tuned. Make it a point to keep an eye on the tachometer when running. Even a beginner can, in time, learn which rpm range constitutes cruising speed, and can try to stay normally on the low side.

The tach can also warn you of impending trouble. Whenever you do run at full bore—and you will, from time to time—a glance will tell you if the engine is turning up to its rated rpm maximum. If it falls short, you have some incipient engine problem that needs examination.

At the same time, keep that seat-of-the-pants expertise you slowly acquire, that sensitivity to lugging and sluggish acceleration. A tune-up may be in order.

## *Operating Tips*

Mention has already been made that four-cycle marine engines must be warmed up when started. You want to get the oil warm and flowing in the galleries, or you will risk damage. Let the engine idle when you start it, and wait maybe five minutes before taking off. And don't forget the earlier advice about idling it down again when you return, before shutting it off. Outboards are exempt, since the oil is already in the fuel.

No engine should be operated for prolonged periods at slow speeds. It has a tendency to foul the plugs. Capacitor discharge ignition may minimize it, but it can still occur. All-day trolling, therefore, can be harmful.

Normally, of course, anyone would be hitting the throttle now and then if only to find a better fishing area, and any carbon beginning to form would burn off in the process. But bear in mind that engines benefit from occasional revs. Avoid continuous low-speed operation; run the engine up once in a while.

This is as good a time as any to point out that four-cycle mills do require a bit more attention in the lubrication department. Combustion by-products can accumulate in the crankcase. It pays to drain and replace the oil and change the oil filter periodically. Your manual will probably make recommendations, but bear in mind that it doesn't hurt to change the oil and filter more often than suggested. There is no replacement for tender, loving care and that great, big, iron "baby" will respond by never letting you down.

One more important operation tip: Try to maintain an efficient drive angle. Both inboards and sterndrives are designed to deliver thrust parallel to the horizontal. Lower unit angle can be adjusted to assure this horizontal thrust from the propeller. This again is where power trim units justify their cost, since optimum trim angle is yours at the touch of a button.

The thrust angle should never be downward (as it is with conventional inboards, where the prop shaft must be angled downward). It's inefficient, and contributes to steering torque problems. It also pushes a boat's bow down, upsetting trim, increasing wetted surface, creating drag, slowing the boat, boosting fuel use in terms of gph, and decreasing range in mpg. That's a very considerable indictment, but it represents the operational evils that befall a skipper who is insensitive to this question.

If you have a choice, rack the lower unit back so the thrust is even slightly upward. This will increase the boat speed, and will improve fuel consumption and range by cutting drag. It's easy to do with power trim, and you can see for yourself how lower unit angle affects steering torque, since you can induce it or eliminate it by adjusting the angle. Without power trim, you have to set the tilt angle on an outboard by changing the "pin." It doesn't take long to discover what pin hole yields the best performance.

## ALL ABOUT PROPELLERS

Your propeller is nothing but a pump without a housing. Its purpose is quite literally to "squirt" a stream of water astern, and Newton's Third Law of Motion applies: for every action there is an equal and opposite reaction. That accelerating mass of water, like the gases jetting from a rocket exhaust, produces thrust that moves the boat forward.

The prop, also referred to as the "wheel," is the heart of your propulsion efficiency. The best boat-engine combination in the world goes nowhere without a prop, and runs poorly if it has the wrong prop. So it pays to know a good deal about propellers, an area far too many powerboat owners neglect. You don't have to be a 24-karat expert, but you should know the basics because you'll need to use them from time to time.

*Propellers are nothing more than pumps without housings.*

## *Useful Propeller Facts*

Propellers are "screws" distantly related to the fastener you use in carpentry or sheet metal. When rotated, they move through a medium.

But propellers aren't threaded. They have a varying number of blades angled in the plane of rotation. The fewer the blades, the less drag and better efficiency, which is why raceboats have props with only two blades. Four blades can produce more powerful thrust, but increase the drag, so most recreational boats have three-bladed props—a good compromise. Slow, displacement hulls may have four or more blades, but we'll be talking only about planing boats.

Props are usually marked on the hub with two important dimensions—diameter, which is obvious, and pitch. Pitch is the distance, in inches on smaller recreational boats but in feet on large vessels, through which the prop would move in a single revolution—like that woodscrew moving through wood. The two dimensions are stamped in that order, and a prop marked "12 × 18" would have a 12-inch diameter, and an 18-inch pitch.

For convenience, prop experts usually combine the two to come up with what they call a "pitch ratio." It is the pitch divided by the diameter. In the case of that 12 × 18 wheel, the pitch ratio would then be 1.5, or 18 divided by 12. A 12 × 12 prop has a pitch ratio of 1.0, and is dubbed a "square" wheel.

Marine engineers have learned, over the years, that certain ratio ranges work best on different hull types. Fast planing craft usually have pitch ratios in the neighborhood of 1.5; heavy planing boats and semi-planing boats do better with square wheels, or ratios in the area of 1.0; and displacement hulls such as trawler yachts and sailing auxiliaries may have ratios as low as 0.5. This is a guide, not a precise rule. Some fast planing boats may do well with only a 1.37 ratio, and race boats may have ratios exceeding 2.0.

## *Tip Speed and Gear Reductions*

You can turn a propeller only just so fast. In time, rotative speed becomes so fast it causes the prop to function more like a blender, wasting power. It just spins in the water, and is fine for making giant daiquiris but not very good for propulsion.

Again, engineers measure this feature. They compute the tip speed, or the speed in miles per hour that any blade tip makes on its rotary path through the water. It's like a racing car on a track. Imagine a tiny racing car on a blade tip, with the circle of rotation as the track.

Tip speed should be limited according to the type of boat and size of wheel. Most outboards, for example, don't produce tip speeds much over 100 miles per hour. Unlimited racing hydroplanes, one of which has exceeded 200 mph on a straightaway, have propellers which reach tip speeds of over 600 mph, but they are specially designed, very expensive, and those boats are probing frontiers of performance.

Engineers installing diesel power in, say, a 40-foot sport-fisherman have a rule of thumb to help select props. They'll start with a square wheel, appropriate to the heavy, semi-planing hull. The rule of thumb (boating is loaded with them) is to begin with a pitch, in inches, equaling half the boat length in feet. Forty-foot boat, 20-inch pitch. But if there are twin screws, common on offshore fishermen which usually have dual engines, you can increase pitch slightly. So they'll start with, say, a 22 × 22 wheel. Then they will *gear the engine down* to keep tip speed within reasonable bounds, which for this type of set-up, would be not much over 60 miles per hour.

By gearing down an engine, engineers arrive at a shaft speed, which is then plugged into the following formula for determining tip speed:

$$\frac{\text{shaft speed} \times \text{propeller diameter} \times 3.14}{1056}$$

Thus if your engine has an assumed maximum speed of 2000 rpms and you try a gear reduction of 2:1, the shaft speed will be 1000 rpm and the tip speed (on a boat of 22-inch prop diameter) will be as follows: $1000 \times 22 \times 3.14$ (which equals 69,080) $\div 1056 = 65.42$. This 65.42 miles per hour would be a reasonable tip speed for a boat with a 22-inch diameter and a 2000 maximum rpm. The 2:1 gear ratio would thus be correct.

Why include all this high-powered mathematical malarkey? Well, it pays to understand it. I know of at least a dozen handy-type men who have assembled their own inboard-powered boats at very considerable savings. They bought bare hulls, in a few cases finding "factory rejects" with minor flaws they fixed themselves and they finished decks and interiors. Then they bought auto engines from a wrecker, and converted the engines to marine engines, using special kits you can buy cheaply. Finally, they installed the engines, all without too much trouble.

But when it came to propellers most were stymied and had to proceed on a trial-and-error basis. Knowing the tip-speed gimmick, and pitch ratios, any man can save a lot of sweat in assembling his own inboard.

One more word on propellers. They should have about a 10 percent clearance above them—and that's a minimum. So taking as an example the man who has now figured he can utilize a 12 × 18 prop on his inboard a-building, he can plan the shaft angle so that a 12-inch diameter wheel will have an absolute minimum of 1.2 inches between the blade tips and the boat bottom—and to be on the safe side it should be 1½ or even two inches. When clearance is insufficient, you get hammering and vibration and hull noises, plus a loss of propeller efficiency.

Even if you never expect to assemble your own boat, the preceding information can be useful in providing background on how propellers are chosen for engines. And if you ever want to compute tip speed "in your head," there's a very simple rule you can apply. Tip speed roughly equals diameter multiplied by three, for each 1000 shaft rpm. In the case of the prop just mentioned, tip speed is 36 mph for each 1000 shaft turns. Anytime you convert engine rpm to shaft turns, even roughly, you can hastily come up with a ballpark estimate on tip speed. For instance, an engine rpm of 4200 divided by a gear ratio of 1.5 is 2800, and 36 times 2.8 equals 100.8. Nice thing about thumb-rules is that they are fast, easy to remember, and you don't need a pocket electronic calculator to work with them.

Now let's return to more immediately practical propeller know-how for the average small powerboat owner.

## *Theoretical Speed*

Propellers also have a theoretical speed, computed easily from the pitch. As explained earlier, pitch is the distance the propeller would move in a single revolution *if it did not slip.*

Theoretical speed is very easily computed. Multiply shaft rpm by the pitch in inches, and divide by that familiar constant, 1056 to find theoretical speed in statute miles per hour. For speed in knots, or nautical miles per hour, the constant is 1216.

To find shaft rpm, you will remember that you must divide engine rpm by the gear reduction. However, there's a small complication. While inboard and sterndrive gear ratios are usually in straight numbers, such as 1.5 : 1, or 2 : 1, most outboard gear ratios are in gear-tooth numbers, such as 13 : 26.

But there's no need to be confused, because a 13 : 26 and a 2 : 1 are the same ratio, meaning the engine crankshaft turns twice for each shaft revolution. Just level the smaller figure in each ratio $G_1$ and the larger one $G_2$ and you can use this simple formula to find theoretical speed *without previously computing shaft rpm separately.* Just use engine rpm, and propeller pitch (P) and here it is:

$$\frac{RPM \times G_1 \times P}{1056 \times G_2}$$

For theoretical speed in knots, use the constant 1216. It's a one-step computation. Let's take that 12 × 18 prop, and an engine turning 4200 rpm tops, with a 1.5 : 1 gear ratio.

Substituting the figures, we have:

$$\frac{4200 \times 1 \times 18}{1056 \times 1.5} = 47.73 \text{ mph}$$

The other way, you would first have to divide the 4200 engine turns by 1.5 to find the shaft rpm of 2800. Then the formula is:

$$\frac{2800 \times 18}{1056} = 47.73 \text{ mph}$$

Either way, the answers are the same.

There's also a rule of thumb (what, again?). Speed in statute miles per hour, *for each 1000 shaft rpm,* approximately equals pitch minus one.

Subtract one from that pitch of 18 inches, you have 17 mph for each 1000 shaft turns; 34 mph for 2000, and 13.6 for the remaining 800 turns (1.7 times 8). Add 34 and 13.6 and you come up with 47.6, or one-tenth of a mile off the more complex calculation.

So remember the easy rule: For each 1000 shaft rpm, statute speed equals pitch minus one.

There you have three ways to figure your theoretical top speed, the speed you would have a right to expect from a propeller that doesn't slip.

But they do slip, so let's look into that subject.

## *Slippage*

All propellers are bound to slip. In fact, they have to or they wouldn't accelerate a mass of water to produce thrust.

Over the years, engineers have compiled some observations that are useful in determining how much slip you can expect from various types of hulls. Inboards are usually well under 20 percent, down to 15 or less, and extremely efficient high-performance inboards may show less than 10 percent slip. Most outboards and sterndrives have slip in the neighborhood of 20 to 25 percent. There are exceptions, of course, but the majority are in this range. Semi-planing craft and houseboats slip 30 to 35 percent. Displacement boats, like trawler yachts and sailing auxiliaries, may have 50 percent slip or more.

How do you find slip?

Time your boat, at top speed, on a measured mile, or any suitable, measured distance. Some simple tricks on setting up your own "trap" to determine boat speed are included in the section on "dead reckoning" navigation, but at this point we'll say only that you should determine your exact top speed by accurately clocking a run on a known distance.

This gives you the true speed, which you compare to theoretical. Here's how you compute slip:

1. Deduct true speed from theoretical to find speed lost.
2. Multiply lost speed by 100.
3. Divide by theoretical speed to find percent of slip.

As an example, suppose we have a boat-engine-propeller combo with a theoretical top speed of 42.61 mph. Suppose we clock it on a measured mile and it makes only 34.6 mph. The difference is 8.01 mph, lost to slip. Follow steps 2 and 3 above, and it comes out to 18.8 percent slippage.

Slip by itself is not a measure of efficiency. But when viewed in context, it is a clue. For a sterndrive or outboard, 19 percent slip (rounding it off) is very much acceptable. You may not do much better, even if you change wheels. For a high-performance inboard, however, it could possibly be improved. All you have to do is maneuver the propellers.

So how do you juggle props? How do you decide whether to go for more pitch and less diameter, or the reverse?

Apply "Hobbs' Rule." It was devised by a marine engineer. It jumped off the paper one day as he was performing some tedious calculations.

Hobbs says that slip should always come very close to 10 miles per hour. Forget slip in percentages, he says, when trying to figure what improvements you may be able to make in performance. Consider it only in miles per hour.

Hobbs says that when slip is under 10 mph, you may benefit from increasing the pitch. If it is over 10 mph, you may need less pitch. Hobbs' Rule happens to fit most recreational boats nicely. So in your theoretical boat with a speed loss of 8 mph, you might improve performance by trying a propeller with more pitch.

Don't forget that pitch and diameter are interwoven. When you increase one, you may (but not always) have to decrease the other. Diameter soaks up more power than pitch; they figure one inch of diameter is worth two inches of pitch. So if you boost pitch, and the rpm drop sharply under that load, you may have to knock off a little diameter to allow for it.

Too much pitch and/or diameter can load the engine so it won't turn up to its rated maximum rpm; too little can allow the engine to exceed the red-line limit on the tach.

The point we've been getting at is that few boats come with perfect propellers.

Any imperfection may become immediately apparent when you load up the boat and find it struggling against stern squat, with the engine lugging somewhat as it strains to shove the heavy load. The tach may even show less than the rated rpm you should expect. This is an instant hint that you should "shift gears" by going to a slightly lower pitch propeller. You may not even lose any speed, since slippage may be excessive with the heavy load; in fact, you can gain speed. The lower pitch is just like shifting a land vehicle to a lower gear. You can pull a heavier load. Knowing how to compute theoretical speed, then obtaining slippage, clues you in on what changes you might have to make to achieve more efficient performance.

As a last item, you can apply anticipated slip in advance to that rule of thumb on figuring speed mentally, and surprise your boat-owning friends by telling them what top speed they can probably make.

Take the rule that speed in statute miles per hour equals pitch minus 1 for each 1000 shaft rpm. Knock off slippage in advance, according to the type of boat. On most outboards it's safe to use the top figure of 25 percent, although if it's a good, clean hull, you know the engine is in fine shape, and suspect the man has some prop-knowledge and is getting the best, you can make it 20 percent.

Just knock off the slippage as you work the speed rule in your head. Take our 18-inch prop example, with 2500 shaft rpm. Speed per 1000 turns is 18 minus 1, or 17. Knock off 20 percent for slip right away, making it 17 minus 3.4, or 13.6. Multiply this by 2.5, and you get 34 mph—within six-tenths of a mile of the measured speed in the previous example.

You'll get a large charge out of telling your friends what top speed they should make, and coming within a mile or two every time. It's easy with a simple rule of thumb.

## *Cavitation and Ventilation*

Turn a prop too fast and it tends to form a vapor pocket on the rear surface of the blade. Incidentally, the "rear" of a propeller is the side toward the bow of the boat; you'd normally call it the front. Just remember it's actually backwards, and the face of a prop is the part that does the pushing.

When the vapor pocket collapses, water rushes in to fill the void, and this water can hammer at the propeller and actually eat away minute particles of metal. This process is called cavitation. In extreme cases it can eat away a blade to the point where it will snap off. Hence the desirability of keeping propeller rpm within reasonable bounds, and avoiding extreme tip speeds.

Those unlimited hydros mentioned earlier, and most racing boats, use supercavitating propellers with blunt trailing edges. They're designed to make the vapor pocket cover the entire rear of a blade, and it doesn't collapse to eat away the metal. Some really high-performance boats can benefit from using such propellers, but they aren't cheap. The subject is brought up because novice boatmen, anxious to get all the speed they can out of a boat, will wander into a shop and ask for a "racing propeller." Ninety-nine times out of a hundred, the average recreational boat will not benefit from using such exotic wheels, even if the skipper can (a) afford them and (b) find one that fits. Stock engines and matching propellers are purposely mated to minimize cavitation. The average small powerboat owner should never have any problem with it.

"Ventilation" is something else again, and the vast majority of people erroneously call it cavitation. In lazy moments, so do I.

If an outboard or sterndrive engine is too high, and you go into a tight turn, the prop is lifted closer to the surface where the water isn't quite so dense, and it may race away, slipping and spinning wildly. It is getting air into it, and can't grab. This is ventilation. It's a point to check when buying a boat and water-testing it, and was mentioned in that section of this book. You won't be happy with such a boat, because it can be a tough problem to cure.

Ventilation can also occur from poor bottom design, perhaps with a keel or skeg that interferes with smooth water flow into the propeller. And it will frequently happen when you get weeds on the propeller—the cure is to stop, reverse the engine, and give it a burst of throttle. It unwinds the weeds.

## *"Cupped" Propellers*

Sooner or later you'll hear someone say he has an "18-inch prop with a cup." Cupping came from racing. The trailing edge of each blade is slightly turned, or dished. It improves the discharge of water, and is usually judged to be worth an extra inch of pitch.

Some propellers come with a cup, others don't, but sometimes you can take a wheel to a prop shop and they'll beat a little cup into it. It isn't expensive, all things considered. It's one way to add a little pitch to a propeller without going to the cost of buying a new one.

## *Propeller Materials*

The vast majority of small powerboat propellers are aluminum, relatively cheap, fairly durable, and available everywhere. There are also bronze props, stainless steel which may be Teflon coated (very expensive), a nickel-bronze-aluminum alloy known as Nibral, and an extraordinarily tough material called Superston.

For most smaller boats, stick to aluminum. Heavy props can tear up the gears of some outboards. The tougher metals came into use when engines became so powerful they could actually turn pitch out of softer alloys. They're mostly for big, expensive, high-performance craft.

Stainless steel, Teflon-coated props are good for outboards they'll fit, but they're very costly—and likely to be stolen by envious boating contemporaries. One man I know gave up buying SST props after having three of them disappear from his boat.

Once you have a good propeller on your boat, take care of it. Don't forget the earlier advice in a previous section about watching it for damage, and periodically pulling it to clean and grease the shaft.

# GETTING THE MOST OUT OF THE GAS TANK

## *How Much Gas Do You Burn?*

Because in these days of rising fuel costs it's important to know how much gasoline an engine will probably burn, the subject was treated at moderate length in an earlier part of this book. In the section on power options when buying, a rough rule of thumb plus a nomogram were provided. The nomogram has been tested, and is quite accurate for gasoline engines of today. You may want to refer to it again. Lacking anything else, it is a useful guide to how much fuel you may be burning.

Note the "Percent Throttle" scale on the left of that nomogram. Now is the time to fill in the blank spaces. Obviously 100 percent is full throttle, 50 percent half throttle. The nomogram had to be designed this way for the obvious reason that engines vary in their rpm ratings. Full bore on an inboard may be 4200 rpm, for example; but on an outboard it may be 5500.

*How much gasoline will you burn?*

Write in your maximum rpm on the 100 percent scale. Then figure the corresponding rpm for the other scale divisions. You wind up with a rough guide to what fuel consumption may be at various throttle settings.

There are other ways to check your fuel use. Nothing beats keeping records on distances, speeds, and fuel purchased. Start out with a full tank. Even on a fishing trip, try to do all your running at the same rpm setting. Avoid idling, and slow-speed running; never open it up to full bore. When you return, top off the tank immediately, noting how much fuel was required. Now do what few amateurs do: break the figures down. Take the distance actually covered, divide by the gasoline consumed, and you have a miles-per-gallon (mpg) figure.

Veterans will tell you that you can't do this, because miles per gallon will vary with wind and weather. This is very true—they vary significantly. But on any extended trip they will tend to average out, just as wind and sea may average out on changing courses. Besides, you need some easy basis for comparison, so work it out to mpg.

Multiply this by your total fuel capacity, and you have a good idea of cruising range on one tank. If you obtain 3.42 mpg then 100 gallons will take you 342 miles.

A smart skipper always keeps his cruising range in mind, and never places full faith in such gadgetry as fuel-tank gauges—especially the remote reading variety. They can malfunction, leaving you someday with bone-dry tanks you thought were still half-full.

All this testing should be done at a good cruising speed, and your figures will be accurate for running at that speed. Obviously you'll get fewer mpg at full bore. And fuel will be wasted at sub-planing speeds. Since it is hugely time consuming to work out a table for varying rpm by actually measuring the gas you use, you can go to other methods.

The small powerboat owner with an outboard and just a few portable, six-gallon tanks has it easy. All he has to do is determine how many miles he can reasonably expect, at a given average speed, on a single tank.

But the guy with a bigger sterndrive or inboard, with a large fuel capacity, can achieve significant savings if he knows precisely what he is burning at any moment. The answer here is a fuel-flow meter. There are several on the market, they're not exactly cheap, but they can pay for themselves in a season on fuel savings alone.

A sensing element goes into the fuel line, and there is a read-out dial for the dash. It reads in gallons per hour. Obviously you must select a model matched to your boat. It's silly to buy a meter that tops at 15 gph when your boat may burn 20 or more.

Divide speed by the gph figure and you convert it to mpg. Now you are equipped to carefully select the best throttle setting for the most economical operation. Thousands of people who own larger craft install fuel-flow meters and put them to good use, conserving fuel first but most of all cutting their fuel costs to the bone.

But a good, fuel-flow meter takes a lot of worry off your mind. Accuracy is probably within 10 percent, at worst, and should be within two percent. The meters serve a secondary function, too. They'll tip you on engine problems you may otherwise never discover—until it's too late.

It's a fact that one spark plug can go sour, and you'll never know it on the average marine engine. Your sterndrive or inboard engine can waste 10 to 12 percent of its fuel when one plug isn't ticking the way it should. You can't often tell by ear alone if you have a bum plug, but it will show up on the fuel-flow meter with suddenly increased consumption. If you have dual engines, with twin meters, and the gph reading jumps on one of them, you've got a sick engine and should check the plugs. If the plugs are fine, then it's another problem, but usually other ailments show up more gradually.

It pays to be aware of your fuel use at all times. Not only can you save money, but you are more sensitive to possible mechanical problems, and can spot them before they become serious.

## *How to Conserve Fuel*

Bits and pieces of this information have appeared previously, and all that is needed here is really a summary.

Reread the section on keeping an engine tuned. It's very important. Keep your cruising speed down. Run at such a speed that the hull is comfortably on plane and moving easily, without squatting or lugging along, but no faster. Combining a tuned engine with sensible operating speeds can carve fuel costs by as much as 25 percent.

Avoid excessive idling. Never, never run at a "mushing" speed. Planing boats are meant to skim the surface of the water. If they are not quite on plane, they mush along. In the vast majority of boats this raises the bow somewhat, puts the stern down. You pull a horrendous wake—a point worth bearing in mind. There is much less wake at planing speeds.

Anytime you are making a lot of wake, you are running at the most expensive speed possible. Fuel is pouring through the engine and producing little mileage. At this point you should either get up on top and plane or slow down to displacement speed, at which point fuel consumption is ridiculously low. So is speed, but that's not the point here.

A small digression may be useful at this point. Like any boatowner, I've been caught with my pants down on fuel, and suddenly found there was less than anticipated; not enough, in fact, to get back.

*Avoid "mushing" speeds, pulling a large wake.*

I always got back. No one ever had to tow me in with empty tanks. Partly I was lucky. But on several occasions it was because habitual checking of fuel warned me in time. By coming off plane and running very slowly, at a no-wake speed—barely making a ripple in the water—I stretched the available fuel supply as far as the dock.

Throttle a four-cycle engine back until it barely moves the boat at four or five miles per hour, and one lousy gallon of gas might stretch as far as 10 or 12 miles. The same boat, on plane at a low cruising speed, might only get four mpg or less.

Another bad habit practiced by most beginners is s-l-o-w acceleration. When you put a boat on plane, you should do so quickly. Open the throttle, jump the boat up in four to six seconds (the range for most smaller powerboats around 20 feet long or less) and then back off to cruising speed. Crawling up on plane wastes gas.

Finally, and repeating advice offered earlier, check your plugs often, replace them when badly fouled, watch your bottom and keep it clean, and avoid running at poor trim angles. If you find that you need trim tabs, install them. Detailed advice is included in the earlier section on "efficient performance."

## *Are Fuel Additives Any Good?*

Unlike automobiles, marine engines receive relatively little use. Gasoline may lie in the tanks for weeks, maybe months, before it has been totally used. Idle carburetors can develop gum deposits.

Additives you may never really need in your car can work to your advantage in a boat fuel tank. Gum solvents, sold under several brand names, may be desirable now and then.

A stabilizer can be helpful. Gasoline goes stale in storage. If you don't use your engine often, add a good stabilizer to the fuel tank. It will prolong the life of the gasoline, and keep it capable of delivering its promised punch and power. Yes, fuel additives can be good in a boat fuel tank. And there is also the question of accumulated water.

You were advised in the section on "your first voyage" to keep your fuel tanks topped off, filling them after each trip, to prevent condensation of atmospheric moisture. Well, it isn't always possible. And human nature being what it is, we are sometimes too tired or too lazy to fill the tanks immediately.

Ultimately water will accumulate. It can stop an engine. If it does, you may have to unbolt and drain the carb and switch to another fuel tank. You can watch out for this possibility by checking your fuel filter. Drip a little gas into your hand, and let it evaporate. If tiny beads remain, that's water, and it's time to take action.

A variety of water absorbers are sold, and your dealer should have some in stock. In any event, you can use alcohol. Any pure, water-free (anhydrous) alcohol will do the trick. Methanol, or isopropyl, alcohol is recommended. It will absorb the water and convert it to a burnable mixture that will go through the combustion chambers. Add one pint of alcohol to each 50 gallons of fuel. As an aside, it works on diesel fuel, too. Maintain that ratio; if you have only 20 gallons, you need less than a half-pint. For 100 gallons, add a quart of alcohol. It'll clean out the water. Of course, if you keep your tanks filled, you'll never have need for it, unless an error is made when servicing the boat—and the boating world is full of such errors.

In my own case, a workman once hosed down the side decks of a boat, and apparently didn't notice the fuel-fill cap was not in place. A lot of water got in the fuel tank. We didn't discover it until too late.

It is not unusual for fuel dock workers to make an error on the fill where larger boats have a water system. They may confuse the fuel fill and the water fill. Either way—whether you have water in your gas, or gas in your water tank—it's a problem. Boatbuilders who are aware of this problem install fuel and water tank fills at wide separations so a careless worker can't make the mistake, though it still happens occasionally. The smart skipper is always watching anyone with a hose in his hand, and makes sure that everything goes in the right place.

You can buy fuel filters that will block water, and they're a worthwhile investment on some boats. But they have a limit. They can be overwhelmed by too much water, and you'll still have a dead engine on your hands.

So to go back to basics, top off the fuel tank or tanks after each trip. Keep them full. It minimizes the problem, and a dose of alcohol now and then keeps the tanks clean of water.

*PART THREE*

# *Operating a Powerboat*

# *YOUR FIRST VOYAGE*

## *First Things First*

Any trailerboat voyage begins at home, when you hitch up. For obvious reasons, make sure the trailer is properly secured to the auto hitch, safety chain in place. Check the boat: Bolsters (side supports) should, if they are the retractable type, be raised under the hull—maybe you had dropped them during the week for cleaning the hull. The strap aft should be brought up taut and checked.

Plug in the trailer lights and make sure they work. Install the rear-view mirrors, if you use the removable type. Check the tire pressures while they're cold. Note the pressure you may need, and add only that differential when you get to a service station. (They'll read higher when hot, so add only the amount indicated when you took the pressure earlier.)

The first time you tow a boat it may be unnerving, but it needn't be. Just drive as if you were at the wheel of an extra-long auto. Swing wide around turns, anticipate braking a little sooner than you ordinarily would.

The dealer should have balanced the boat on the trailer when you bought it, ensuring adequate tongue weight (about 10 percent of the total load). If not, you would have noticed it when you brought the boat home. It would have "hula danced" on the highway, gently jogging from side to side. With smaller boats, however, you can unbal-

Left: *Check tiedowns and trailer hitch, when starting out.*
Right: *Usually you can tow boat with engine down. But tilt it up if you know you'll cross rough railroad tracks, or run bad roads. Lower unit can be damaged.*

*Tyro trailer-boatmen can learn a lot by practicing backing in a deserted supermarket lot on a Sunday.*

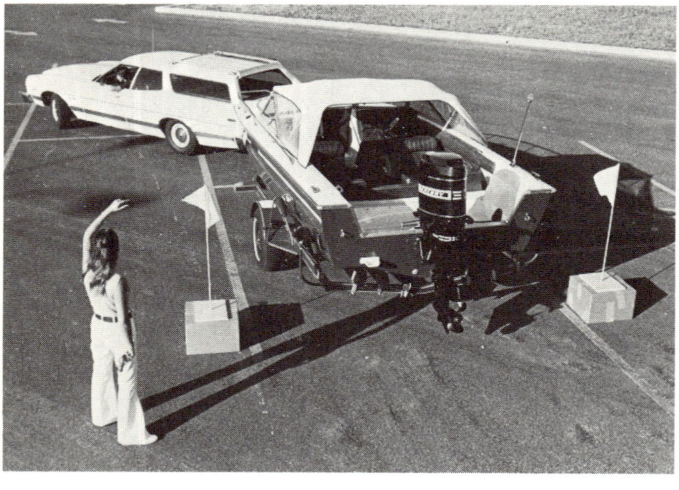

ance the rig, yourself, when you stow ice chests and portable fuel tanks aboard. If it jogs from side to side under tow, stop and shift some weight forward.

If you don't already make a habit of watching your rear-view mirror almost constantly, start doing it now. You want to know what's coming up behind you, want to watch out for tailgaters, and should avoid creating a long line of traffic on a two-lane highway. Don't drive too slowly. Aggravated autoists may try to leap-frog past, and could create an accident.

## *At the Launching Ramp*

When you pull into a ramp area, your first problem will be backing the trailer. It will prove difficult, since you'll have to reverse your normal steering habits. You turn the auto wheel left to back the trailer to the right.

*Backing a trailer is a knack. Just steer with the "bottom" of the wheel.*

*Chocks prevent car from rolling down ramp.*

*Tilt engine, insert drain plug, have bow line ready and push off.*

Keep this trick in mind and it will take all the work out of it: Steer with your hand on the bottom of the wheel, push left, and the trailer will back left. Push right, and it will back to the right.

Never oversteer. If you do, you'll "jackknife the rig," as truckers would say; and you'll have to pull forward, straighten out, and start over.

If the ramp is crowded, you should prepare for launching before backing down to the water. Remove the tie-down straps, and tilt the outboard or sterndrive unit up. Usually, when there's no line waiting to launch, this can be done when you have backed almost to the water's edge.

When ready to go, back the trailer into the water. In most cases you won't have to submerge the hubs, so try to avoid doing so.

Block the auto wheels, especially if you have a heavy boat. You can buy special blocks, some that will fold flat, or you can make your own. You may even find old rocks laying on the ramp. They're community property, and used freely by all to block their wheels. It is very rare, but on some steep ramps it has been known to happen: the trailer will slide down into the water, dragging the auto with it. So block the wheels, and set the parking brake.

Tilt the bed, if you have that kind of trailer, rig a bow line, and shove the boat off the trailer into the water.

Some people unhook the boat from the winch cable before pushing the boat off. Others like to leave the cable on the boat until it just goes off the trailer. Then they unhook the eye, and latch it somewhere on the aft end of the trailer. It's ready for instant hook-up when you return to reload. Take your choice.

Someone should be tending the bow line, and can pull the boat off to one side—to a finger pier if there is one—and tie it up while you park the trailer.

Two hints when you park: first, remove the winch handle and stow it in the locked car. People have been known to help themselves if they lost their own winch handle, and some odd-ball characters have, at some ramps, stolen handles and blandly sold them back to their furious owners. Secondly, get in the habit of checking the trailer rollers when the boat is off the bed. Spraying a little lubricant from time to time (not every trip) will keep them from ever sticking.

## Reloading the Boat

When you return to the ramp, reverse the procedures. Back the car and trailer down to the water, guide the boat up to the trailer, hook up, and winch it out. It's really simple.

But watch these points: if there is a cross wind, have someone hold the stern in line. They may use a boat hook, stand in the water, or position it with a dockline to the stern cleat. It's all but impossible to load a boat unless the hull is kept in line with the trailer, and that includes the so-called self-aligning rigs with guides.

And don't forget to block the auto wheels again when you haul the boat out.

One final word, saved for last to lend special emphasis: Always check the transom drain plug, if your boat has one. Many a sorrowful boater has launched his craft with the plug out, and found it half-sunken when he returned from the parking lot. Launching and re-loading are easy, once you get the hang of it. Remembering the drain plug isn't. It has probably happened to almost every trailerboat owner at least once.

# SAFETY ON THE WATER

## What to Do Around Docks

The first thing you'll do with your new boat is tie it up. Details on this aspect of seamanship will come later, but this much is important now: you basically use two lines, a bow line and a stern line, each leading ashore from the appropriately located cleat.

In the case of the stern line, always cleat it on the side of the boat furthest out from the pier, the "outboard" side. It will hold the stern in close against the pier, neatly parallel.

The normal instinct is to cleat the stern line "inboard" or on the cleat nearest the pier. In nearly every case, this won't hold the boat snugly parallel; the stern will drift slightly out. Cleating stern lines to the outside is the mark of an experienced boatman. You might as well start out with that image.

We'll talk about docklines later, but the point to bear in mind on your first trip is to keep the loose line on the boat. Don't let great loops of extra line lie in spaghetti-like coils on the pier. Not only is it sloppy seamanship, but it's a hazard to the unwary who may trip overboard. You should have an eyesplice in the end of the line, which goes over the piling on the pier. Cleat the rest on the boat, at the proper length for the situation, and coil it neatly.

Before starting the engine, check the fuel system. Make this a habit on any boat. Be sure your outboard tanks are properly hooked up, pump up pressure on the bulb in the line, and make certain no tank is sitting atop a flexible fuel line—it can shut off the fuel flow. With sterndrives (or inboards) open the engine box or hatch, sniff for fuel fumes. If you have a bilge blower, operate it for five minutes. Be sure all fuel-line valves are open. More than one amateur skipper has worked and sweated to start an engine he thought was balky, when his problem was in the fuel system.

When you do start up, be sure the shift is in neutral. (On most engines there's a safety interlock and you can't start in gear.) Open the throttle slightly. Choke it if you lack an automatic choke. Start the engine. Let it idle—especially four-cycle engines—several minutes to warm up. It's extremely important with four-cycle mills, to get the oil flowing and assure proper lubrication.

Only after your engine is running do you take in your docklines! Amateurs too often take in lines and then start up; and if the engine doesn't fire up it's embarrassing.

Then comes the magic moment: shove off! You may push off from the bow, slip into forward gear, and move away. Sometimes you'll back away in reverse. Either way, go slowly when in a dock area. Any mistakes should come out as mild bumps rather than torn bow rails and shaken-up passengers.

This is the time to point out that boats definitely do not steer like autos. On land, an auto tracks around the front wheels. The front of the car steers. With boats, you steer by the stern. Get in open water and put the wheel hard over, at slow speed, and you'll see the stern swing around first, pointing the bow in the desired direction.

Keep it in mind, always. Remember, when you put the wheel over, your stern will swing out in the opposite direction. This is why beginners, who try to pull away forward from a parallel dock, will bang the stern into the pier. Turn away gently, or back away. Boats are easier to control in reverse (outboards and sterndrives, anyway) and handle better.

You'll see this when you dock. With outboards and sterndrives, which steer by a vectored thrust—the propeller direction is turned, and you have "power" steering—docking is a lead-pipe cinch. Come in very slowly at an angle to the pier of about 30 degrees. Shift in and out of neutral if you must, to hold your speed down.

When the bow is just about to touch the pier, shift into neutral and quickly turn the wheel so the propeller is *aimed toward the dock.* Then shift into reverse, and give it a little, brief bit of throttle. You will take the "way" off the boat, bringing it to a stop; and at the same moment you will pull the stern in so it lies alongside the pier. Shift back to neutral immediately.

Docking an outboard or sterndrive is extremely simple, thanks to that power effect in the steering. With an inboard, which has a rudder,

*Docking an outboard, in two steps: 1. Angle in to pier.*

you must keep water flowing past the rudder or you will have virtually no steering at all.

Single-engine inboards, with right-hand propellers (the propeller rotates clockwise when seen from astern), are very difficult to dock. Because of propeller torque they will go easily to port—forward or astern—but poorly to starboard. For this reason you should try to dock them with the port side to the pier. Angle in slowly, go into neutral. As the bow is about to touch, put the helm hard over toward the pier, go into reverse just as in an outboard. You'll halt the boat, and the stern should come in close enough.

Try it starboard side to, and the boat will be balky. For the same reason, if you must back into a slip with a single-engine inboard, set yourself up so you back down to port rather than to starboard.

Some boats—and most sailing auxiliaries are typical—won't back down at all to starboard! This is what makes outboards and sterndrives delightful to handle around docking areas.

When it comes to shutting down an engine, you can kill a two-cycle kicker the minute you tie up the boat. But if you have a four-cycle engine, raw-water cooled, and are using it in salt water, let it

*2. Turn engine and reverse to pull stern in.*

idle for five minutes. You want to cool it down gently before turning it off. Otherwise salt can come out of solution in the cooling passages and cause later trouble. Idling also distributes oil evenly. Never race an engine before shutting it down. It can suck in a little water via the exhaust, and cause trouble.

With any engine, always keep an eye on the instruments or idiot lights. Even outboards can develop a clogged cooling intake. With four-cycles, watch water temperature and your oil. Plastic bags, tossed overboard by the zillion in America's waters, seem to have developed an affinity for cooling water intakes on engines. The result can be some costly damage.

## *After Clearing the Docks*

Once clear of the dock area and other boats, get the boat up on plane. Shove the throttle open smartly, all the way, and ease back as the boat rises and levels.

Avoid full-speed operation in any boat. It's costly in terms of fuel consumption, hard on the engine. Two-thirds throttle is usually plenty. You'll get the feel of it after a while. Stick to what boatmen call "cruising speeds." High cruise is just as much fun as running flat-out. You'll acquire a seat-of-the-pants feeling in time.

## *Fueling Procedures*

The most important factor in safe boating is to remember that your gasoline-powered engine uses an explosive fuel. So always be careful when fueling. If you have an outboard, take the portable tanks out of the boat and set them on the pier. It's safer than fueling in the boat and risking spillage. When filling outboard tanks, incidentally, *never pour the oil in first,* adding the gas later. It isn't a matter of safety, but deserves mention at this point. The oil will puddle on the bottom, and the pick-up tube will grab fuel too rich in oil at first and too little oil later. It can mean everything from fouled plugs to scored pistons or other damage.

Pump in a little gas first, then add the oil. Swish the tank around, fill with gas, and make sure it is mixed. With fixed tanks, you can add oil intermittently as you pump in gas. It must be well mixed.

When fueling sterndrives or inboards, open the engine box or hatch, shut down all electrical equipment, turn off the galley stove (if it was operating). Obviously, engines should never be running. Top the tanks, and don't let them overflow. Spillage in an inboard is potentially hazardous if it gets in the bilges.

Before starting any engine, use your nose. It's the greatest fume detector ever devised. Keep hatches open, operate the blower, check the lines to be sure nothing is leaking, and *then* start the engine. This is normal routine, and should be faithfully followed. If gasoline weren't explosive, your engine wouldn't work. Treat gas with respect, and you'll never have an explosion or fire.

An important point: gasoline can be too rich in its mixture with air to burn in an engine; and while few people realize it, the mix can also be too rich to explode when in the bilges.

This is exactly why you will often read newspaper accounts of a boat exploding shortly after it has pulled away from the fuel dock.

There are fumes in the bilges or engine compartment, and they are too rich to explode. But when the boat begins moving, the ventilation ducts admit air and the mixture is leaned down to the point where a spark can set it off.

Very obviously, this can never happen if you use your nose and sniff for fumes. If present in enough quantity to explode, they are always detectable. Air out the boat thoroughly, and make sure you have no leakage that can cause the fumes to accumulate.

As a matter of reassurance, records indicate that only one out of every 80,000 outboards will have a fire or explosion in a year. The ratio for inboards and sterndrives is about one out of every 2,500. People could make them as safe as outboards if they would use their noses and a little more common sense.

Always slow down in tight situations, such as narrow, curving channels, especially creeks where you can't see around the bend. You should also take it slow when passing fixed objects close aboard and when passing moored or drifting boats. Give everyone else a wide berth. Don't buzz other craft, beaches, bathers, and navigational markers.

In narrow channels, when boats pass each other going in op-

*Never permit bow-riding. It can be fatal.*

posite directions, both should slow down. Slow down when hitting the large wakes of yachts or commercial vessels, coming all the way off plane until you are experienced. Veterans know that some boats can take a fair wake at full bore, and will usually behave better than they would at half-speed, but this feeling comes with experience. You'll also find you can cross large wakes more tolerantly at a sharp angle rather than hitting them head-on.

Always keep a sharp lookout ahead! Failure to do so is the reason for most collisions, especially with fixed objects. It sounds silly and obvious, but too many people take their eyes off the water ahead, sometimes for long moments. Watch for floating objects that can cause trouble if you hit them.

Keep your boat trimmed. Exercise your right as "captain," and move passengers from side to side so the boat is level, not heeling or listing. In small boats, too much weight forward holds the bow down, slows the boat, and can make it wet in bumpy going. Too much weight aft makes it ride harder, if a conventional hull design. It can also be faster, with a little more weight aft, but don't overdo it.

Never overload a boat. Overloading, combined with allowing a boat to get into poor trim, can cause accidents, especially in rough water.

Never permit anyone, under any circumstances, to ride on the bow with legs hanging over the stem. It is very dangerous, and people are killed every year when they fall overboard and are struck by the whirling propeller. The tragedy is that they are usually children, whose indulgent parents permitted them to ride in this dangerous location. The Coast Guard considers it reckless operation, and may cite an operator if they see a case of bow-riding.

Your first trip will probably be a short one. Most people tend to restrict their horizons when new to boating. It's natural and also wise to stay close to home port until you get the feel of the boat and acquire a little experience in handling it under a variety of conditions.

## Float Plans

When you are ready for more adventurous trips, consider that handy feature universally known as a "float plan." All boating authorities recommend it. Fliers file "flight plans" and this is essentially

*Leave "float plan" with someone before making a long trip into relatively empty waters.*

the same thing. Should you experience an engine breakdown, run out of gas, or get into some other problem, a float plan saves you much time and embarrassment.

If you were making an offshore voyage, such as from south Florida to the Bahama Islands (they're only 50 miles from Miami), a float plan is an absolute must.

Here's all you do: Write down a complete description of your boat, including its number. List the people who will be aboard, and the safety equipment you may have. List also your trailer, with its license number, and your car, and where it will be parked.

Leave this information with a friend or neighbor, and tell them when you plan to return. If on a long passage over open water, arrange to call them and tell them you reached your destination safely. This way, if you do not return or make contact on schedule, they will know to notify the authorities, such as the Coast Guard, so they can look for you. With the float plan, they know what they are looking for, and about where to start looking.

They'll probably try to find the trailer first. Wise old Coasties have found, from bitter experience, that sometimes a man on a fishing trip is fishing for something else. More than once a missing angler has been located in a bar with a girl friend. The Coasties don't inform a worried wife about such details.

More seriously, it's smart to leave the vital stastistics with a friend or neighbor when you take off on a more venturesome voyage. But if you do your homework (reading this book is part of it), have a good boat, good engine, spare means of propulsion, proper tools and spare parts, and practice ordinary maintenance, you'll probably never have a moment of trouble afloat. It's that simple.

## *Personal Flotation Devices*

Another word about PFDs is in order with regard to safety. Always make nonswimmers, especially children, wear life vests on board. Wise skippers prefit jackets to their guests and show them how to don them. This is required by law on cruise ships, but few skippers do it on private craft, perhaps because they don't want to scare the wits out of their passengers. In any case, you should at least show them where the vests are stowed, especially if on a long trip, or if and when it turns into a nasty one with worsening weather.

Put on a lifejacket in a bad situation, like running a rough inlet; and make everyone else wear one, too. It's a sad fact, long-known to the Coast Guard, that most deaths from drowning could have been avoided if the people had put on their PFDs when they encountered bad water and weather.

As a last word on safety, try and avoid such situations. Normally you can. Check the weather forecasts, and don't go out in high winds or rough seas. Even big lakes can be nasty in squally weather. Coastal inlets can be dangerous in a storm. Avoid them. And study the later section of this book on boathandling in rough water. There's a knack to it, as in everything else.

*Make children and nonswimmers wear their PFDs at all times.*

*It can get busy out there.*

# THE RULES OF THE ROAD

Any time you get out of bed in the morning you face some sort of hazard. You can trip over the cat, cut yourself shaving, fall in the shower, even become involved in a fender-bender on your way to work.

As an odd but interesting aside, a survey was made of people who get involved in boating mishaps, and it was found that nearly all of them were accident-prone on shore. If you're a klutz, then you're a klutz, and all hands have to live with it.

Boating, basically, is very safe. The equipment, by and large, is well engineered. Accidents caused by mechanical problems or other failures of boats and their control systems are rare, and in most cases even these could be avoided if the boatman practiced regular preventive maintenance.

Statistically most accidents are the fault of the operator. To slay a few dragons, the average operator involved in an accident is a mature man in his thirties and has had at least 500 hours of operating experience. The mishap usually occurs late in the afternoon on a clear day.

Tyros can take considerable comfort in this revelation, gleaned from Coast Guard statistics. Editorial writers and other scribblers of obtuse commentary are apt to blame beginners for everything that goes wrong in boating. The truth is that the novice is characterized by timidity, and he rarely gets into trouble. Familiarity breeds potential hazard.

There is no substitute for knowledge backed with responsible

*The sound boatman is always equipped for any eventuality. This skipper carries spare prop, among other items.*

judgment. The odds are overwhelming that our mythical 35-year old skipper with 500 hours at the helm lacked one or both of those qualities. Safe boating, in the end, is common sense and courtesy.

You could easily be a safe boat handler without any of the information that follows, if you possessed common sense in a large measure and were constantly courteous to other boaters. It's that simple. But it doesn't hurt to learn some of the essentials, the rules of the road. Once mastered and religiously adhered to, they make boating the safest and most enjoyable of all leisure time activities.

Let's start with what landsmen might refer to as the "traffic laws."

There are traffic laws at sea, and they are codified in immense detail. Russian trawlers, American naval aircraft carriers, cruise ships of Panamanian registry, Coast Guard cutters, and your relatively tiny, 18-foot outboard, are all subject to the "Rules of the Road." They're published by the Coast Guard in a thick booklet carrying the identifying number, "CG-169." You can obtain a copy from the Coast Guard.

Luckily, the whole book can be condensed into certain basics for small powerboat operators. You can virtually skip the part massively titled, "International Regulations for Preventing Collisions at Sea," since you logically enough may never go to sea.

Should you ever put land out of sight astern, as you can when running 50-odd miles from Miami to the Bahama Islands, then just give all freighters and other large vessels a very, very wide berth and you'll never have to concern yourself with the laws.

More pertinent to most boatmen are the Inland Rules of the Road, which will vary somewhat from one area to another—western rivers, Great Lakes, and intracoastal zones. However, the essentials will be condensed in the following, and we'll break it down into particular traffic situations you are likely to encounter.

## *Passing Other Boats*

Often you will be passing other boats, either head-to-head, (opposite directions) or in overtaking situations where you overtake the other boat, or it overtakes you.

The rule is simple. Keep to starboard (the right) whenever safely possible. That means, in most cases, you pass a boat going in the opposite direction port-to-port — your left sides facing each other.

But this is not a hard-and-fast rule! Veteran skippers of commercial craft on the busy Intracoastal Waterway (which runs from New England to Texas) are often bugged by amateur boatmen who buzz across their bows so as to pass port-to-port. The idea is to keep to starboard, but not to make a fetish of it, for there obviously can be times when it is wiser or safer to pass on the other side.

How do you know which is best, and how do you trade opinions with the other skipper? Whistle signals. In an earlier section on equipping a boat, the point was made that all craft 16 feet and up must carry whistles or horns. Let's provide the details, first by explaining boat "classes."

All boats under 16 feet are called "Class A" and needn't carry whistles. Boats from 16 to 26 feet are Class I boats, and must have hand, mouth, or power-operated whistles or horns audible at a half-mile range.

Class II craft are from 26 to under 40 feet, must have hand, mouth, or power-operated horns audible at a range of one full mile. Class III boats, 40 to under 65 feet, must have one-mile power horns only. Why? Because there is a "code" of whistle signals that signify intent on the part of one skipper, and a responsive affirmation from the other. You can even argue with your whistles.

It should be obvious to all hands that most small boats don't customarily use whistle signals. They are usually going too fast, pass each other before you can dig out the tooter and give a toot or two. But bear two things in mind: First, you are required to carry horns or whistles on boats that are 16 feet long or larger, and, secondly, if an accident occurs, and you didn't sound a signal, you may be held at fault.

With that much in mind, let's learn the simple signals.

## *Whistle Signals*

One l–o–n–g blast: Means you are backing out of your slip or berth. It warns other skippers of your action. It is also used on rivers when you approach a bend beyond which you cannot see. One long blast warns an invisible approaching vessel, which is supposed to reply in kind.

One short blast: Means, in a head-to-head or meeting situation, and in an overtaking situation, that you wish to pass the other vessel on your *port* side. It has another use, to be explained later.

Two short blasts: Means, in the same meeting or overtaking situation, that you wish to pass the other boat on your *starboard* side.

The two signals are very easy to commit to memory. The word "port" has one syllable, calls for one whistle blast. "Starboard" has two syllables, and the signal is two blasts.

Three short blasts: Means your engines are in reverse. It is also used to signal for the opening of a bridge.

Four (or more) short blasts. A danger signal. You can blow four times to "argue" with the other skipper, advising him not to carry out his signaled intentions.

In very rare cases, four blasts also signals a bridgetender to open a span that might be on a restricted schedule. Bridges near cities may be limited in their openings during vehicular rush hours, for example. If you have an ill or injured person aboard, or similar vital reason why you cannot wait for the permissible scheduled opening, four blasts will open the bridge on an emergency basis. But make sure the emergency is genuine. The tender will report your name and number.

It's really simple. Most small boats never use the one long blast when backing out of a berth, or even rounding a bend in a stream. You aren't even supposed to use the other signals unless there is the possibility of collision. So don't go about merrily tooting your horn all day. Occasionally, however, you will meet or pass another boat in a narrow channel. Circumstances may put you close together. Under these conditions, it's advisable to slow down and use whistle signals.

Here's how the system works: You are passing another boat, and wish to pass port-to-port. You sound one short blast. If the other skipper agrees, he confirms by repeating you, sounding one short blast in reply. Go ahead and pass. *If he does not agree,* he will sound the danger signal of four blasts. Do not try to pass port-to-port. If he sounds two blasts *after the danger signal* it means he thinks you should pass starboard side to him. You acknowledge and pass.

Never make what are called "cross signals." Never answer one blast with two, or vice versa. Always use the danger signal as a correction, then sound the signal that seems proper for the channel conditions.

It's a fact: You can overhaul a slower boat in a narrow channel, coming up on his starboard side. You sound one blast because you wish to pass with him on your port side. But he can see ahead, and he may be able to spot a shoal or some other hazard not visible to you. *Any boat being overtaken* has the right of way. So if he sounds the danger signal, you must drop back and not try to pass. If he sounds two blasts, then it means you are better off going around him so he is on your starboard side. Do so.

This pretty much covers meeting and overtaking situations. Remember that signals are not used unless you will be passing the other boat so closely that there is some risk of collision.

*Passing port-to-port, or keeping to the right. Larger craft would use whistle signals, in this case one blast on horn.*

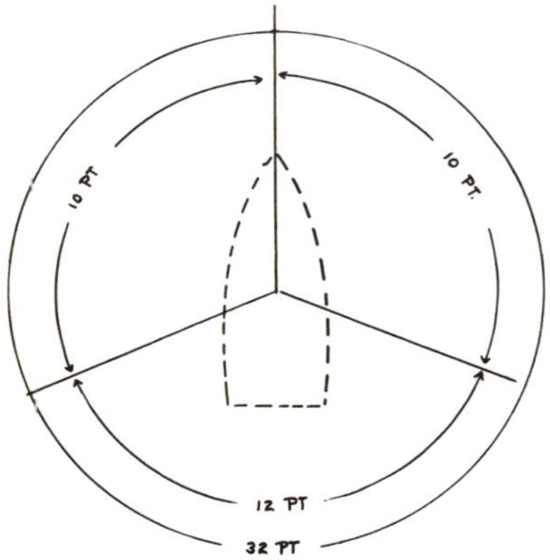


*Sketch shows how circle is divided into "points."*

## Crossing Situations

On more open water, boats are often crossing each other's courses at an angle. Here the rules are a little different.

You'll notice that virtually every powerboat built has the steering station on the starboard side. There's good reason for this. It allows good visibility over what is described as the "Danger Zone."

This zone covers an arc from dead ahead to "two points abaft the beam." Seamen divide a circle into 32 "points," each one an arc of 11.25 degrees; a 90-degree angle would be eight points, and that's on the beam—straight out to the side. So the danger zone covers an arc of 10 points, or 112.5 degrees starting from dead ahead. See the sketch.

This danger zone is on the starboard side only of every boat. And any boat, crossing your path, coming along *in that zone,* has the right of way. In seaman language, it is the "privileged" craft, and you are the "burdened." The burden of avoiding the other boat lies on your shoulders. Keep clear.

The privileged boat, on the other hand, has the obligation of maintaining course and speed. To make changes in either can only confuse the burdened skipper. No whistle signals are required, but the privileged skipper can sound one, short blast to signify his understanding that he does have the right of way and will maintain course and speed.

To sum up powerboat right of way, any boat being overtaken has

*Boat approaching from starboard (right) has the right of way.*

the right of way; any boat crossing the track of another, coming out of that danger zone, has the right of way. It's automatic, spelled out in the Rules of the Road, and you can't change it. But don't rigidly insist on your right of way if it will obviously cause a collision. In the final analysis, you are supposed to do everything in your power to prevent collision—which is what the Rules of the Road are all about in the first place.

## What About Sailboats?

Never, never exchange whistle signals with sailboats. They have their own rules. Under normal circumstances, sailboats *under sail alone* have the right of way over all powerboats. Give them a wide berth. It goes without saying that you pass with care, in narrow channels, whether meeting or overtaking; and slow down so your wash doesn't trouble them. With a light, planing outboard and safe clearance, you can go by on plane. Such small powerboats produce less wake at cruising or full speed than they do when you back off and they fall off plane.

At mushing speeds, described earlier, they pull terrible wakes. Avoid such speeds around other boats. That's common courtesy, and also shows you've acquired experience.

Sailboats, however, do not have the right to claim privilege in a narrow channel, when the other boat may be unable to maneuver easily within the confines of that channel. This change in the law was made a relatively few years ago, and not every sailor knows it yet.

Sailors can be as rude as powerboatmen at times, and you may encounter some screeching, shrill juvenile in a windjammer who'll scream at you, "Don'tcha know sailboats have the right of way?"

The answer is that they don't. Not always. They must not embarrass larger craft unable to maneuver easily in narrow channels. Otherwise, they do have the right of way over powerboats.

Another point to bear in mind about sailboats is that if their engine is running, even if all sail is set and drawing, *they are legally considered powerboats.* They obey the same rules, and whistle signals may be exchanged if needed.

Bear in mind, however, that sailing craft of any size are not at all like powerboats. Their skippers deserve far more courtesy than they get from the average powerboat owner. Don't make heavy wakes around them, give them as wide a berth as possible, don't buzz them, and keep an eye on them. A sailor may have to "tack" or suddenly change course 90 degrees or a little less, for reasons that may not be apparent to a powerboatman. Give him room. He'll appreciate it.

A proper exchange of courtesy would go far toward easing a sort of traditional tension that has long existed between "ragmen" or "blowboat" skippers, and "stinkpotters," as the two types of skippers call each other.

## *Navigation Lights*

Now we come to a toughie, for even in CG-169 there are inconsistencies and contradictions. The rules on navigation lights need revision and updating.

But again we can simplify a mass of detail. Meticulous students are advised to get a copy of CG-169 and study it if they wish to investigate the finer points. Luckily, we can largely confine ourselves to smaller boats.

A few generalizations first: Federal law, as already explained, requires "running lights" on boats used after sunset. Most small powerboats come with lights already installed. If they are lacking, you do not break any federal regulation *unless* you run the boat after dark.

However, check your state laws—your dealer should know, although most dealers are better at marketing than interpreting state boating statutes. Florida, for example, requires running lights on all water craft, power or sail. That includes airboats operating in the vast Everglades. The theory is that a boat may be stranded out after dark because of mechanical problems, or the skipper's sudden whim to stay a little longer, lingering over an active fishing hole and ignoring the setting sun.

It's this writer's own opinion that no boat should be without lights. They need not be permanently installed. You can buy "skiff" lights, for example, battery-powered, that can be mounted only when actually needed. This is perfectly legal, and on some boats it is an adequate solution.

Any small boat should have an emergency white light, which can be an electric lantern or flashlight. Rowing boats and canoes should have them, for flashing as a larger boat approaches, to warn the oncoming skipper. Small sailboats should have such lights to shine on the sail, although in Florida they would technically have to have conventional running lights. Again referring to Florida law, stricter than many other states, an emergency white light is required on the grounds that conventional, fixed running lights can fail, and a substitute would be desirable.

Navigation lights come in different colors, and will vary by the class of boat, although all small boats are virtually the same.

## *THE RED AND GREEN BOW LIGHTS*

Most important are the so-called sidelights, or red-green combinations at the bow. The red light shines on the port side, which is easy to remember: red is the color of port wine, and the red light is on the port side. The green light goes to starboard.

Each colored light covers an arc from dead ahead to exactly 10 points aft, *or two points abaft the beam.* Go back and reread the part about the so-called "danger zone." You will realize, then, that if any boat is approaching you in a crossing situation, entering your danger zone, *you will see his red light.* Since the other skipper is coming in on your starboard side, *he will see your green light.* It's automatic traffic control. Traffic lights gone to sea. Red for stop, green for go.

You cannot see the wrong light. They were designed to cover only the arc of the danger zone. If you see both colored lights, the boat is coming directly toward you. If you see neither light, the boat is ahead of you and going away, although you may be overtaking it and should keep an eye on it.

If you see only red, or only green, you know automatically which boat has the right of way. See green, and you are privileged. See red, and you are burdened. It is beautifully simple, and the system predates the traffic lights for motor vehicles on land.

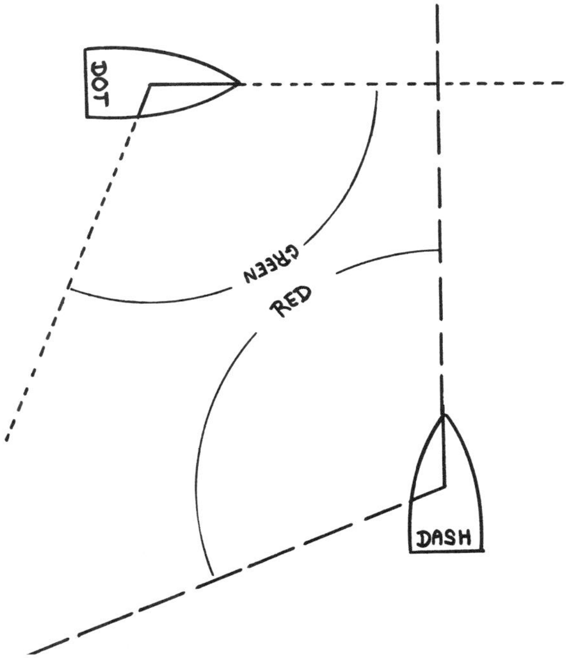


*Red-green lights provide automatic traffic control. "Dot" skipper sees red light from "Dash," and skipper of latter sees only green light.*

These colored lights may be combined into one unit and placed at the bow of any boat under 26 feet long. The rules become a little more complex on larger craft, and we'll explain that later. Suffice it to say that a combination bow light meets the law on any boat under 26 feet—and that's why you see the combination so often.

A word of advice: The lights are supposed to be shielded so they do not "cross" over the bow, showing a glint of green on the port side and red to starboard. Obviously this defeats the purpose, and can lead to accidents. Better quality lights are screened, and won't lead to confusion.

As a practical matter, however, when a boat approaches you at night the two colored lights in many cases seem to blend and produce a sort of off-color white. Only when the other boat alters course slightly will one light then dominate—red or green, as the case may be. This is a decided weakness of cheaper combination lights.

Another warning: when you change a burned-out bulb, make sure you replace it with an identical type. Go by the make and number of the bulb, and if you can't get the same one, buy the equivalent. This also applies to white lights. Installing the wrong bulb, one not recommended by the manufacturer, can change the arc of visibility and even range, or distance at which it can be seen.

## *WHAT ABOUT THE WHITE LIGHTS?*

The sidelights (or bow-light combo) are most important, but the rules require white lights, too. They provide some idea of the size and relative direction of the other boat. A stern light is required on all powerboats, and a special "range" light may also be required. But exactly what kind of white light is carried depends on whether your boat is equipped for Inland Rules or International Rules.

Most small boats are carrying Inland Rules lights, since the vast majority are used on lakes and rivers. But you'll see International Rules lights on many boats along the coasts and in areas where you can cruise in the open sea. Operating in Mexican, Canadian, or Bahamian waters would make international lights acceptable. You can use international lights anywhere inland, too. But you can use inland lights only inland—never offshore. Keep that in mind if you live somewhere near a coast, and figure you may someday cruise to, say, the Bahamas. Coastal charts show a line of demarcation, usually running offshore from headland to headland, where the International Rules take over.

Now let's look at the lights, by boat class and type of rule:

## *INLAND RULES*

Boats under 26 feet long require:

1. A 32-point white stern light, visible two miles all around the horizon.

2. A combination red-green bow light, 10 points on each side, visible one mile. The separate sidelights are also legal, but not mandatory.

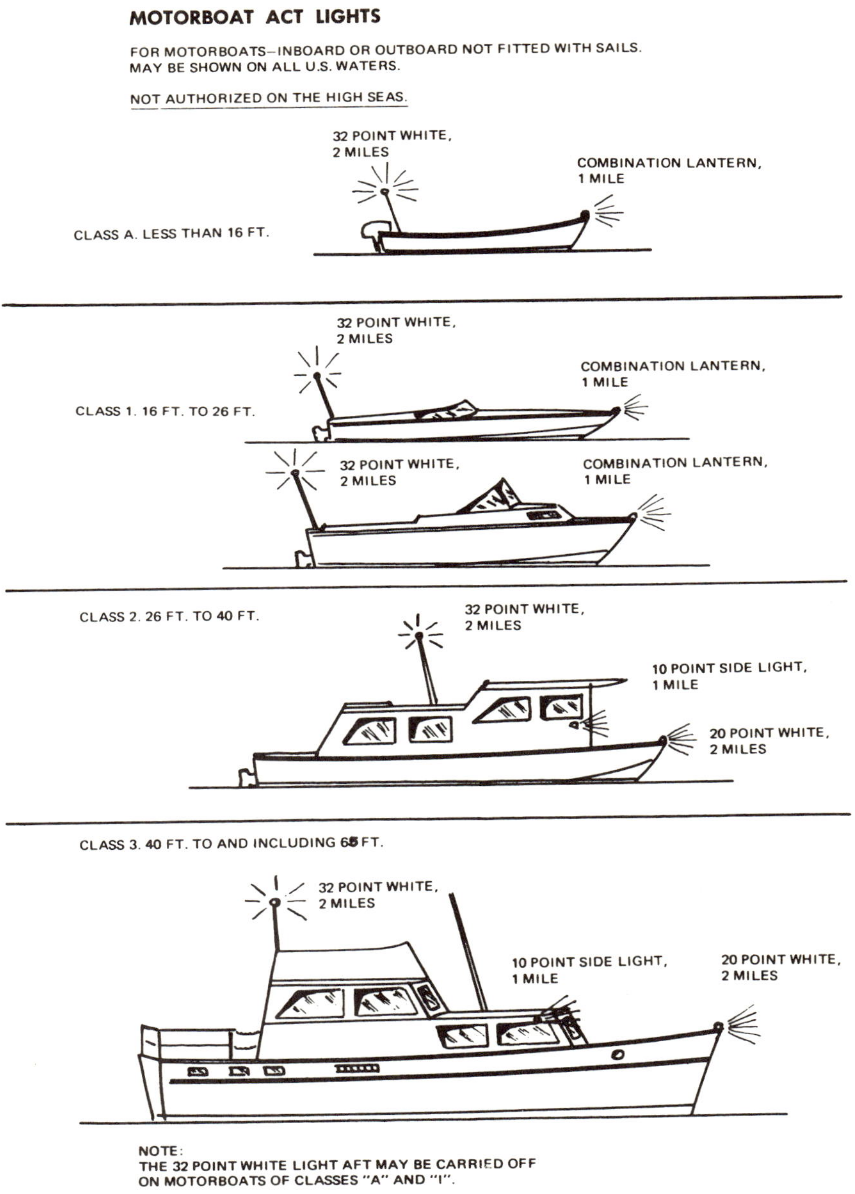


*Motorboat Act lights.*

**INTERNATIONAL RULE LIGHTS FOR MOTORBOATS**
**INBOARD OR OUTBOARD**

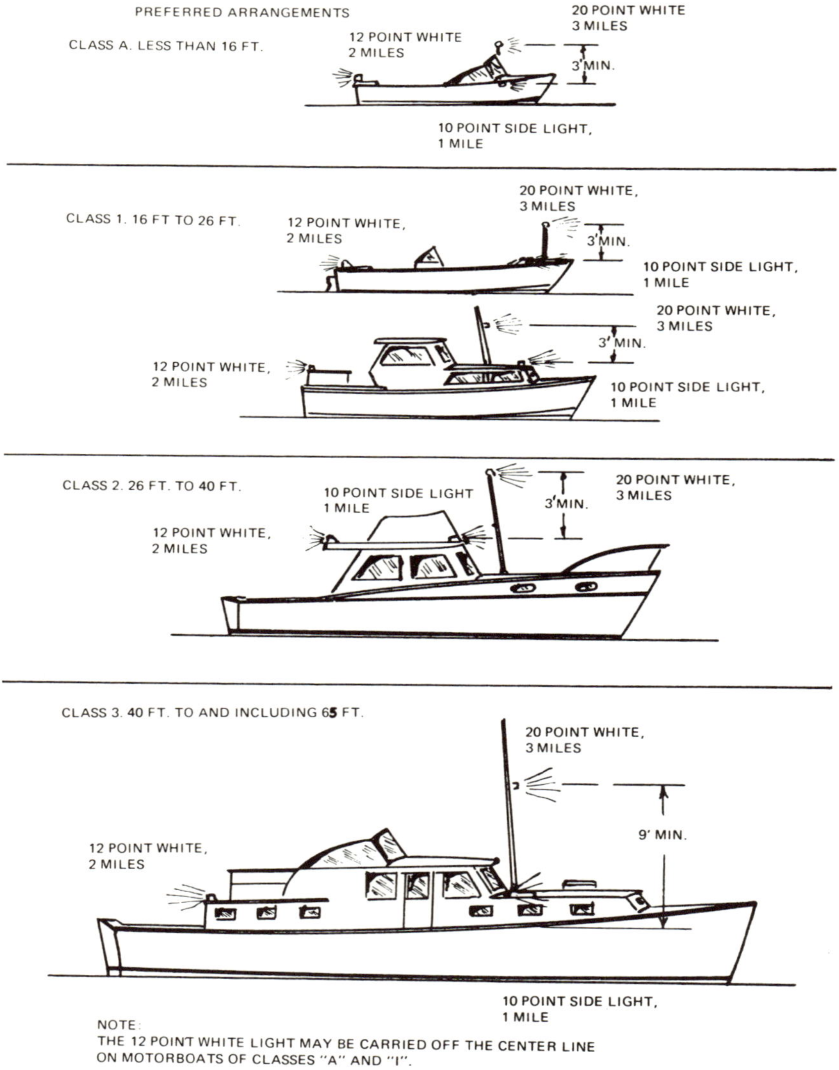


*Preferred International Rule lights.*

## INTERNATIONAL RULE LIGHTS FOR MOTORBOATS INBOARD OR OUTBOARD

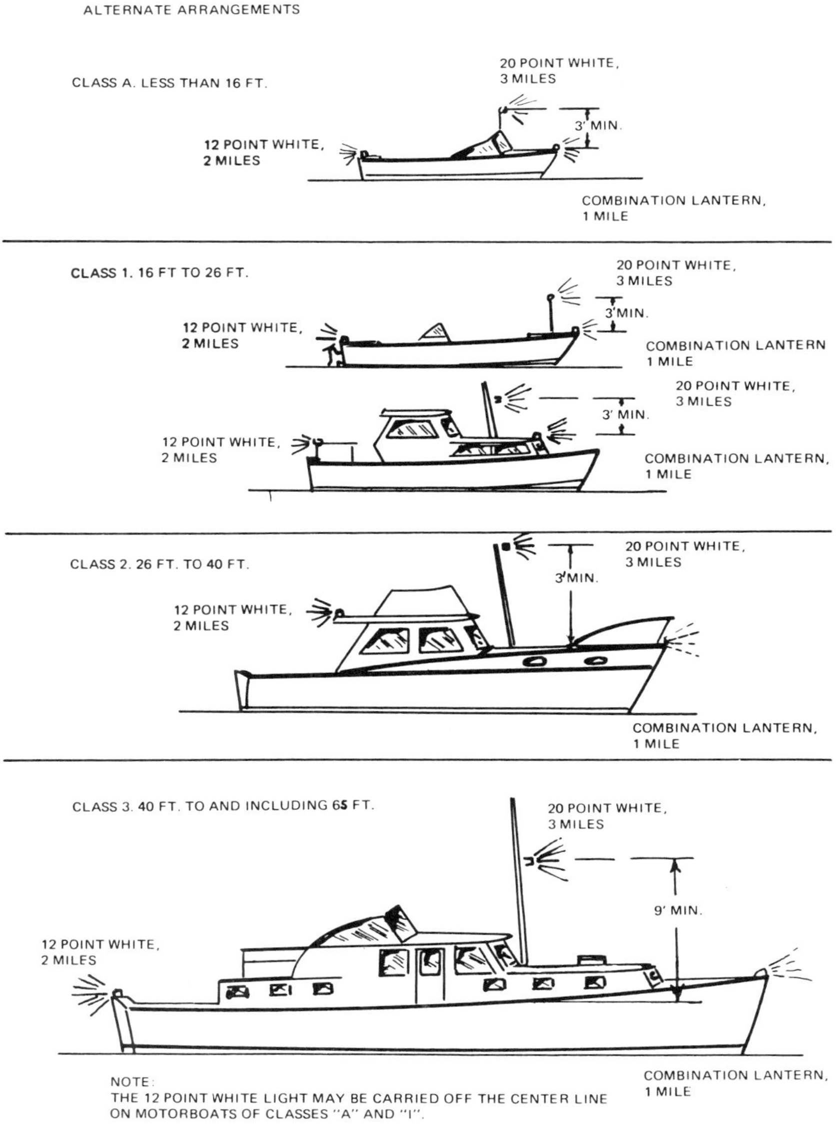


*Alternate International Rule lights.*

Boats over 26 feet long require:

1. A 32-point white stern light, visible two miles all around the horizon.

2. A white, 20-point bow "range" light, also visible two miles, and positioned lower than the stern light.

3. Separate sidelights: a 10-point red light to port, a 10-point green light to starboard. The combination light is not legal.

## *INTERNATIONAL RULES*

Boats under 65 feet long require:

1. The red and green lights, either separate or in combination. A combination red-green light is legal under International Rules on boats over 26 feet long. Range is one mile.
2. A 12-point white stern light aft, visible two miles.
3. A 20-point white bow light visible three miles.

In the case of boats under 40 feet, that bow light must be a minimum of three feet above the colored lights. On boats 40 feet and up, it must be at least *nine feet* above the colored lights.

The vertical separation rule causes problems on smaller powerboats. To meet the three-foot requirement for the average boat in the 20-foot range, give or take a few feet, the bow light invariably must be located so it may blind the skipper at night. The rule was reached under international agreement, and it is fairly obvious that other nations don't have the huge recreational boating fleet America possesses.

On many small boats at night, the only thing the operator can do to maintain his vision is turn off the 20-point light. This is patently illegal. The only observation I can make is that I have turned it off more than once in order to see what was ahead of me. But I never did so when other boats were nearby. This confession is made in full knowledge that it won't please the Coast Guard.

When the 20-point light is off you are still protected by the red-green lights and that 12-point stern light, which is precisely what sailboats are supposed to show at night when under sail alone—Inland or International—just the colored lights and a 12-point stern light.

(Sailboats under power must show the same lights prescribed above for motorboats.)

Just to make the cheese more binding, and to illustrate some of the conflict in the rules, the Motorboat Act of 1940—which is still in effect, as amended—has a different set of sailboat rules.

In their version, motorboats under sail alone need show only the red-green lights. They are specifically forbidden to show white lights but must carry an "emergency" white light, such as flashlight or electric lantern, to show in time to prevent collision.

So to repeat, I don't see any great flaw in shutting off a 20-point white bow light if leaving it on blinds me. I would do so, however, only under the safest circumstances, when cruising under a full moon, at modest speeds, in open water, and not around other boats.

None of the foregoing should be construed as advice to the reader that he break the law by turning off his own lights, at any time.

## *The Flaws You Find in Lights*

Sadly, not everyone in the marine industry understands the rules, and you often see careless installation of lights. One example is the installation of separate sidelights, red to port, green to starboard. Sometimes you see the colors on the wrong side of a boat. Occasionally sidelights are installed below the sheer, on the part of the bow where the topsides flare outward. This aims the lights at a downward angle toward the water, which means that they just can't be seen at the required one-mile distance, especially from the bridge of a large commercial vessel. You will also see, although rarely, such oddball instances as sidelights installed so they shine straight upward. So when you buy a boat, give the lights a close check.

And a final note. Some years ago the Coast Guard tested a number of lights. They discovered a flaw that is still extant, at least as this is written. On low-voltage, direct-current systems, no bulb exists on the market that will provide the required one-mile range of visibility on a green side light.

When you consider all the flaws that just might exist, you realize that extra care must be taken when operating a powerboat after dark.

The other fellow may have some kooky light installation, have his colors reversed, or a bad bulb on the green side. Never take anything for granted. Don't be *fearful* of running at night in marked waters. But do be cautious.

## *Anchor and Other Lights*

Whenever you anchor, unless in an area specifically set aside and so marked on charts as a special anchorage, you must display an anchor light.

It is supposed to be hoisted to the masthead, and should be visible all around the horizon. If you don't have a mast, the anchor light must be as high as possible.

*Anchor light is required on boats anchored overnight.*

In many small boats the only available light is the 32-point, white stern light (Inland Rules). The problem here is that the stern light can rarely be seen from dead ahead of the boat. Visibility is often blocked by the windshield, the convertible top, or by people aboard. This is true even when the boat is underway.

For this reason you see more and more small boats with International Rules lights. It is possible to buy a special 20-point white bow light, with an additional 12-point segment lighted by a separate bulb. There's a two-position switch. Pull it to the first stage, and the 20-point light goes on for running. Pull it to the second stop, and the remaining 12-point segment goes on, and you now have a 32-point anchor light. Because of the three-foot vertical separation rule, this light usually, even on small boats, is higher than the windshield. It serves as a very adequate anchor light indeed.

As a last word on lights, don't forget the earlier advice to carry an emergency light of some kind. Always be sure you have spare fuses and spare bulbs aboard. And as explained in the maintenance section, take your navigation lights apart from time to time and clean them. They're a vital part of boating, and a necessity after dark.

# WATCHING THE WEATHER

To paraphrase Mark Twain's famous observation on weather, "Everyone talks about weather but few people watch it."

You can't take weather for granted when you own a boat. A lot of beginners in the outdoor world—hunting, fishing, boating—quickly find that their pleasures depend to a great extent upon weather. In time they develop an instinct, and pick up some basic meteorological knowledge. Old-timers can virtually sniff the air and announce that rain is likely.

For those who are not tuned to Mother Nature, it's best to start out by habitually checking official forecasts provided in a communications deluge by the National Weather Service. You can't turn around without hearing or reading about the weather.

This point should be made immediately: Weather is a highly volatile phenomenon, always changing. *Every weather forecast is obsolete the minute it is made.* It behooves the outdoorsman to bear this in mind and make a habit of checking the forecasts. A fine day may be predicted as you sip your morning coffee. But by noon the Weather Service may have detected changing conditions, and a later forecast may predict something like "locally heavy squalls."

Forecasters are extremely capable professionals, and massive weather systems—like cold fronts and low pressure systems—are carefully monitored. The catch is that these phenomena can slow down, speed up, stall, or dissipate.

Take a thunderstorm, for example. Maybe the morning forecast predicts something like, "partly cloudy, with widely scattered showers and thundershowers during the afternoon and evening."

Sounds fine. But to the guy who gets caught in a thunderstorm, it is far from fair. Winds in a small storm can easily reach 50 or 60 miles per hour; rain can come in the form of a blinding downpour. And one thunderstorm can breed others. A dying storm sends out masses of cooled air, which flow under surrounding warm air, starting an upward movement. When enough heated air rises, another "cell" can form. So a fair morning and reasonable forecast can degenerate into a mass of squalls. It pays, therefore, to "watch the weather."

## *Start with Official Forecasts*

The best source for weather forecasts comes from a chain of government radio stations. All are on VHF (very high frequency), which means maximum range is about 40 miles. There are two frequencies, 162.40 and 162.55 Megahertz, but they are usually referred to as "Weather One and Weather Two."

There is no point in giving a count of the stations or a list of locations, because new stations appear every year and a list would be obsolete by the time it appeared in print. Suffice it to say weather stations are located near every major boating center, from Hawaii to Maine, from Alaska to Florida.

If you install a VHF marine radiotelephone in your boat, you can add one or both crystals and receive the instant weather forecasts, provided, of course, there is such a station in the region and you are within range of it.

The market is flooded with small, portable receivers capable of receiving the weather stations. You can find them at discount department stores, drugstores, and every other kind of outlet. The salesman should know if there's a weather station nearby, and should be able to tune it at the counter. If you have any doubts, call your nearest Weather Service office and ask. Also inquire about the probable range.

Once equipped with such a radio receiver, you have the weather at your fingertips. Broadcasts are continuous, 24 hours a day. It's a recording, but regularly updated, and weathermen break in at any time for emergency announcements of locally severe storms. You absolutely cannot get caught with your pants down, if you have one of these radios and use it habitually.

Another source of up-to-the-minute forecasts is the commercial radio station. Some periodically relay the Weather One or Weather Two broadcasts. Most depend on teletype links to the local NWS office. But a warning is in order here: Occasionally a rip-and-read disc jockey will hastily provide obsolete weather. Forecasts on the teletype are timed, and are not to be broadcast after certain hours, but some radiomen occasionally miss the warning.

Newspapers obviously cannot be up to the minute, but most provide weather maps recent enough for a knowledgeable boatman to interpret for himself. Basically, of course, all you can observe on a weather map is systemic weather. Television weather is, on the whole, pretty good, but lies somewhere between newspapers and radio since it is not presented as a rule except on a strict schedule.

There are other sources, but not of much concern to the average small powerboat owner. The Coast Guard, marine radiotelephone stations—colloquially known as "ship to shore" radio—and some Federal Aviation Agency radiobeacons, provide weather forecasts at intervals. But your best forecasts are from the weather radio stations. None can touch "Weather One" for detail and timeliness of broadcasts.

*Weather affects every boatman. You can expect showers from vertically developing clouds.*

## *Keep an Eye out to Windward*

You should develop a certain "feel" for the weather. People have been doing it for millennia. Check your Bible, Luke 12, 54: "And he said also to the people, When ye see a cloud rise out of the west, straightway ye say, There cometh a shower; and so it is."

The one area where you depend on yourself is in the development of purely local phenomena such as showers and squalls. You can see them by merely keeping that "weather eye out to windward."

Especially watch the west. Biblical people weren't wrong. Most of our weather tends to come from the west—but by no means all of it. Watch the west, and the northwest, but don't ignore other quadrants. You can spot bad weather a long way off.

When a cloud begins to thicken, to grow vertically, it promises a small shower. If it continues to thicken and grow, you may be watching the birth of a thunderstorm. In most powerboats, you can run around them, move away, evade them. But watch them carefully. When they grow and grow and grow, soon the entire area will be covered with squalls. One thunderstorm, as noted earlier, can breed others. That's because, at one stage of a storm, cooler air flows downward and spreads out radially in all directions. If you are on the upwind side of a storm, the cool air flow bucks the prevailing wind, canceling it out. This is the "calm before the storm," but it doesn't necessarily mean the squall is moving your way. Winds on the downward side are increased by the flow of air, and it can become gusty. The same phenomenon can be noticed during the formative stage as air flows into the chimney of the growing storm. Winds will be higher on one side, all but canceled out on the other.

Thunderstorms are tricky monsters. Avoid them. If they grow into a solid band, run for safe harbor.

Pay particular attention to predicted wind velocities, and "small craft-advisories." The NWS stopped using the old term "small-craft warning" years ago. Today they are advisories, and you use your own judgment, considering carefully your skill, your boat, and the area where you will be going.

## When You're Caught in a Storm

Everyone gets caught sooner or later, but make it later if you are just starting out. With experience, and a little common sense, you can handle a hard blow.

If you can, try and outrun a blow. Careful weather watching makes it possible. But if caught on wide open water when the wind starts to rise, and seas begin to build up, follow these rules:

1. Slow down. Don't try to maintain planing speed. Come down

*Quartering into the seas may produce a lot of spray but it is much more comfortable, and easy on the boat.*

off plane, and resign yourself to slogging along. Don't punish the boat and people aboard.

2. If it gets really bad, head into the seas at a very slight angle. Back off on the throttle until you are only maintaining steerageway. This is called "heaving to," and you would be amazed at how well a boat can ride out a squall when you follow this course. In deep water the motion is quite comfortable. In shallower water seas will be

steeper, sharper. But heaving to is the only answer. Keep the bow toward the seas at a small angle.

3. Engines sometimes quit in squally going. Spray gets into the ignition system, ailing engines decide to quit. Debris in the tanks gets through the fuel filter and stops the engine. In such case, rig a sea anchor. If it's really rough, have one ready before you need it.

A sea anchor, or drogue, is very handy. Commercial types are like little parachutes—cone-shaped bags with a bridle, to which you secure a long line, like your anchor line. A trip line goes on the apex of the cone, so you can "upset" the sea anchor when the emergency is over and haul it in backwards, with no drag.

Streaming a sea anchor holds the boat's bow into the wind and sea. You'll drift downwind, of course, and better have "sea room." It's no joke to be caught on a lee shore—onto which the wind is blowing and the seas pounding.

(As an aside, to dispel confusion, if you are tucked up under a lee, it is the shore *from* which wind is blowing. But if you are on a lee shore, it is the shore *toward* which the wind is blowing. The first is safe and desirable; the second potentially hazardous in a hard blow.)

You can buy sea anchors in better marine stores. Smart seamen carry them, since they collapse for easy stowage. Just buy one large enough for your boat. A sea anchor two feet across the ring will hold any small powerboat easily. You can jury rig one in emergencies. A plastic ice chest, for example, might serve—anything, even a bundle of junk, a convertible top, a portable outboard fuel tank, might work—but put your trust only in the manufactured variety, on small boats. If you lack experience, you may get too flustered to rig an adequate makeshift.

Let's make a couple points very clear about sea anchors: You would need one only on large bodies of water that can turn really rough in a blow—open bays and sounds on the coasts, and the offshore seas, and really large lakes. You would need it only if you lost power. And you would need it only if you got careless about watching the weather.

So if you exercise any reasonable care, you'll never be in a spot where you'll stream a sea anchor. Nonetheless, it's a good idea to know what they are.

## *Running Inlets*

Coastal fishermen love to seek their quarry offshore, which means going to sea—usually via an inlet. Running inlets is a tricky business, and it's a good idea to store a few general inlet facts in your memory. They are generalizations, which can be dangerous, but local sources can advise you of any peculiarities worth knowing.

These facts are generally true: When the tide is ebbing, and the wind is onshore, inlets can be rough. The wind is bucking the outgoing tide. Even on a moderate day, some inlets can turn nasty at full ebb, late in the day.

Why late in the day? Because the "sea breeze" usually increases during the day. A sea breeze is caused by the sun heating the land mass. The rising warm air must be replaced. Cooler air from the sea moves in as a breeze. As the day wears on and the land becomes hotter, the sea breeze gains velocity. Mind you, this may not occur every day, nor in every area, but it's a rule to remember.

Another rule to remember is that inlets are often calmer near the edges than they are in the center. Check your inlet and see. Often you can work your way in or out near the edge and avoid the steeper seas in the middle.

Few people venture out an inlet when it is nasty; not if they are in their right mind. But it is not unusual, as noted, to return from a day offshore and find the inlet distressingly bumpy—even on an otherwise pleasant day. So you must know how to run an inlet.

If the seas are rolling in easily, a fair distance apart, you can "ride them in." Put your boat *on the rear slope* of a sea or swell. Adjust your throttle to keep it there. Do not go too far up the slope. You could go over the crest, and "pitch pole" or cartwheel end over end down the front face. It has happened to small boats when the seas are large enough. Do not fall back into the trough between the seas, or onto the front face of the next following sea. Stay on the rear slope of a sea and follow it in. It'll take you to calmer water. Don't fret even if the sea breaks into white, foaming surf. Calm water lies just ahead, when this happens.

I've taken 40-footers in through inlets covered with huge rollers, with breaking crests, exactly this way. Once it was so rough a 50-footer ahead of me got caught by a following sea and broached, or swung sideways. Luckily, it did not capsize—which is what you can expect if a following sea picks up your stern, throws it to one side, and rolls you over.

Stay out of the trough. Don't broach. You can avoid this, if you sense your stern swinging, by steering against it—just as you would steer an auto against a skid. If your stern moves to starboard, turn the wheel to starboard and hit the throttle a bit to straighten the boat out.

Believe it or not, it can be an exhilarating experience. I've known people to run inlets for the fun of it, once they learned just how it's done.

If you have a displacement hull, or lack power—maybe you're limping in on an emergency kicker—you meet the inlet problem by creating drag. On a mild day stream the anchor line astern, with each end on a quarter cleat to form a loop in the water. It'll create drag, hold your stern to the seas, and thus prevent you from broaching and capsizing.

If it's nastier, a sea anchor does an even better job. Just stream it astern. It'll hold you on a steady heading, prevent broaching, and reduce the possibility of swamping as a sea breaks over the stern and floods the boat. You might take some water, but not as much as if you broached and rolled in the trough.

Bear this final note in mind. Even on good days an inlet may be bumpy at or near the mouth, where the wind and tide produce "standing men," or seas that don't really seem to move much. But it can be very nice just outside. So sneak around the edges and enjoy. Avoid panicking and trying to turn around right in the bumpy part. Ninety-nine times out of one hundred an inlet poses no problem. But that hundredth time, watch out.

A very important point should be made: The preceding section may appear, to the casual reader, to sound like boating is a constant invitation to disaster. It isn't. You can go through a lifetime of boating, in small powerboats, and never face a serious emergency. And that's what this book is all about: it explains what *can* happen to the unknowing; it shows how you can *avoid* it; it advises you how to *meet* it if you are unexpectedly caught.

# WHEN IN DISTRESS

The Rules of the Road help you avoid collisions. Knowing the weather helps keep you out of rough water. Common sense and very basic seamanship teaches you how to handle the bumpy going. The previous section showed you how to avoid swamping and capsizing. Despite all this knowledge, you may someday find yourself in distress. When that day comes, keep cool and try to remember what you're about to read.

First, make everyone aboard don their PFDs. You too. If you do tip over, remember that new boats 20 feet and under must have flotation. They won't sink. So stay with the boat! Do not try to swim to shore. Rescuers can find a boat a lot easier than a bobbing head. The only exception would be small bodies of water where shore is only a relatively few yards away, and there's an easy beach rather than rocks.

If the boat has capsized and is floating bottom up, it's hard to hang on. So keep yourself busy rigging lines, if you can get at your docklines—and they should be handy when you face the problem in the first place. Running a line from bow to stern helps all hands hang on somewhat more comfortably.

Follow the right procedures and no one will suffer. You'll have an adventure story to relate later.

## *Proper Distress Signals*

"Distress" is a funny word, since a small powerboat owner who exercises common sense will never face any greater distress than running out of gas or breaking down—and even that shouldn't happen.

The usual procedure for people who run out of gas or suffer an engine malfunction is to stand up and start waving frantically at passersby in other craft, who usually wave back in total misunderstanding and proceed gaily on their way.

At only a few hundred yards distance any sort of standard "wave" can be easily mistaken for a friendly "hello, there," and will earn only a similar hand-flap in response. About 15 years ago this factor was recognized and a sort of standard distress signal was devised.

It calls for standing up in the boat, or on the bow deck, and facing any boat passing in the near distance. Raise your hands straight out to your sides, drop them, repeat over and over. Don't flap like a bird. Do it fairly slowly, holding the arms out straight to the side. Bright-colored cloth, like orange rags or red bandanna, aids visibility.

The point is to do something out of the ordinary, that cannot be confused for a conventional, cheery "hi, there" type of wave. It is more apt to make someone approach to ask what's up, rather than zoom on past. As such, it makes sense. And while mighty few small powerboat owners know the accepted signal, you should stick to it if you want a tow back to dock.

There are other sorts of distress signals. Your need to carry them depends upon many factors: what kind of water you are on, how open it may be, distance from shore, your own skill, impending weather patterns, and more. You must judge for yourself what to carry, if anything at all.

Personally, I don't think you need anything at all on small bodies of water where you are nearly always in sight of the dock or launching ramp, or on confined waterways with much traffic. But it's another cup of tea if you wander well off shore on large bodies of water, or on the coasts.

Here are the other signals, with an assessment of each:

1. *Flares:* Red flares are commonly sold as distress signals. To begin with, they are utterly useless in the daytime. They should be used only at night, and even then only when you think someone is looking your way or is actively searching for you and approaching. They're hard to see at any great distance.

Flares do come in rocket form, to be shot from a gun. Guns increase the range of visibility, but the flares last only a matter of seconds until they fall in the sea. Parachute flares cost more, maybe too much more, but do last longer. Like hand-held flares, they should be used judiciously, not fired wastefully.

Hand flares can be in real cheapie form, with a packet of paper matches in the "kit" to light the flare, or a better version with a tape that ignites the flare when you yank it. Buy the better types. Paper matches are virtually worthless for lighting flares in the wind and rain.

2. *Orange Smoke:* This signal is obviously meant to be used in daytime, and is no good at night. This is why you should have both flares and smoke and never just one. And get good-quality orange smoke.

Orange smoke signals emit huge volumes of thick, brightly hued smoke, visible great distances to a searching aircraft. On the surface, range is limited—as with red hand-held flares—by the curvature of the earth. On small boats it's rarely more than a few miles, unless there is a big wind, which disperses smoke quickly.

So don't ignite either type of flare on the basis of sound. If you hear an airplane or another boat, wait until you can see it clearly. If you can see the other boat, the people on it can see you and your flares.

3. *Dye Markers:* In a class by themselves, but strictly for daylight use, dye markers consist of a packet of yellow sea dye that can turn blue water into a sharp yellow-green patch that stands out for many miles, at least to searching aircraft. On ocean racing craft sea dye markers are often tied to PFDs, and are part of all survival kits packed with inflatable life rafts.

Anyone using wide open water, where searches may be made by plane such as in some national parks, coastal zones where the Coast Guard may be involved, and large state waters involving Marine Patrol forces, should carry sea dye marker packets. They're a big help. Especially if you happen to sink. A man in a PFD is mighty hard to find, but it's a lot easier if he is sitting in the middle of a large patch of discolored water.

4. *Canadian Surface-to-air Signal:* This is an orange flag with a black ball and black square on the long axis. It is recognized as a distress signal, is meant to be displayed flat on deck or cabin so it is plainly visible to aircraft overhead. Obviously it is carried only by more sophisticated and knowledgeable seamen working offshore. However, it should be mentioned. It has its values.

*A signal mirror is the best distress signal for small boats.*

5. *Signal Mirror:* Of all the distress signals, none is as versatile or universally known as the common mirror. Special mirrors for signaling were devised in World War II. They have peephole sights so you can aim the sun's reflection at a target, such as a distant plane or boat. Signal mirrors can be found in any good marine store, except possibly those in the hinterlands of boating. No boat should be without one. On any water.

The signal mirror with sight is best, but you can get by with a common hand mirror. How do you solve the sighting problem? Use this trick: Hold your arm out, fully extended, toward the distant boat or aircraft that you wish to signal. Make a fist, and *hold your thumb upright.* Just touch the target with the tip of your thumb. Hold it on the target.

Now flash the sun's reflection with the mirror at the target. Keep the sun flashing over your thumb, which in turn is "on target." Move the mirror very slightly up and down, back and forth, to flash the sun's reflection over your thumb, and you can count on plenty of flashes hitting that distant aircraft or boat.

Do not be discouraged if it is a little hazy. A mirror will still work. It takes heavy cloud cover, or darkness, to stop it cold. And don't feel blue if the sun is in the "wrong" direction. Obviously you need to have the sun in some quarter where you can reflect it with a mirror. If it is behind you when you face a distant boat or plane, then you can't use a mirror.

Or can you?

The answer is that you can—with a "secondary reflector." Have someone else face the sun, and reflect the sunlight *into the mirror you hold.* This way you can make the mirror flash a signal even when the sun is on the wrong side of you.

Obviously, also, substitutes for mirrors can be improvised. The bottom of a tin can can be pressed into service. However, the real thing is so cheap there's little reason not to have one or two on board.

Incidentally, don't worry about not knowing Morse Code. It's almost impossible to send a readable message in Morse with a handheld mirror anyway. All you have to do is flash light on another boat (or searching aircraft) to draw their attention.

Every boatman has had the experience of glinting sunlight flashing off the windshield of a nearby boat. Maybe at first you thought someone was signaling. Usually it is only coincidence, for it is not repeated over and over, as a distress signal would be. Such flashes can be seen to the very limit of the horizon, not very far away. If your height of eye is, say, six feet you can see only to the horizon, which thanks to the curvature of the earth is just 2.8 nautical miles (3.2 statute) away. Someone else, with a six-foot eye height, can spot your signal an additional 2.8 nautical miles farther on, but the total distance for such eye heights is only 5.6 miles. You can't see an inch farther until you raise the eye height on one end or the other. Blame the earth, which is a lot smaller than people think. On a lake that is one mile across, the center will be about two inches higher than the shores because of the earth's curvature. It is that measurable.

There are other so-called distress signals, including some that have international recognition such as international code letters, firing guns, and other devices. Some are informal, but work. A man I know once drew attention to his disabled boat (he had to wait for nightfall) by knifing open a buoyant cushion, pouring outboard fuel into it, lighting it, and dropping it overboard.

There is one signal that has no international recognition and never will, although it is popular in fiction. That's displaying the national ensign upside down. Maybe a U.S. citizen would notice that the U.S. flag is upside down, but such tricks have no standing in the world community because many, many national ensigns look the same when inverted. You can't tell them apart, rightside up or upside down. Seamen never invert ensigns to draw attention. There are other ways, that work better.

## *Marine Radiotelephone*

Your greatest aid to safety afloat is a marine radio, provided you do your boating within range of a Coast Guard station that monitors the so-called "distress" frequency. Such radios are highly recommended for boats used in extensive cruising along coastal waterways, or fishing offshore or in bays and sounds. They should be considered a must if you go far offshore for any reason.

Under regulations that took effect in 1972, any new marine radio licensed for a boat must be a type called "VHF" for very high frequency. It is also a frequency modulation radio, or "FM," but those two letters are usually dropped.

VHF has many virtues. It is almost totally free of static, even from the twin bugaboos, engine ignition and lightning storms. It has a lot of room. There are 39 channels for communications, plus two more dedicated to weather (Weather One and Weather Two, described earlier). Power is limited to 25 watts, and when working in harbors or crowded areas, you are supposed to cut this to one watt with a switch required by law. Range is therefore a little restricted.

As a result of all this, VHF doesn't suffer from overcrowding, at least not yet. You have room on the airwaves to talk, or get out a message related to your situation, such as being out of fuel, or whatever. It is a great safety aid, a special line tied to shore, an invisible

*Two-way radio is link to shore.*

link to land. The one disadvantage is the limited range. Older radios, often referred to as MF or medium frequency, AM for amplitude modulation, and DSB, for double sideband (it was all three at once), had good range. And that became a problem. As more and more ship stations (the official word for it, even though the radio might have gone on a small outboard) went into service, the airwaves became a crackling, static-filled, jabbering rat's nest of intertwined conversations and interruptions. You couldn't hear yourself think.

Hence the ordained switch to VHF. There are still some old "MF, AM or DSB" on boats, but they have to be torn out and thrown away by Jan. 1, 1977, the deadline for total conversion. Meantime, should you buy a boat with MF radio, bargain the price down. Under the law, the radio license cannot be transferred to a buyer. The owner can keep the radio and move it to a new boat he buys, at least until 1977. But he can't sell the radio.

That leaves you with VHF. Plenty of good sets are around on the market. Range is limited to line-of-sight (here we go with the horizon bit again) or, if the antenna tip is only six feet high, a distance of 2.8 nautical miles—and you saw those exact figures a short while ago. If another antenna is six feet high, then range between the two radios is 5.6 nautical miles.

Now, nobody goes for a low antenna, and most are double that height, even higher on larger craft. Shore antennae of the Coast Guard and those ship-to-shore telephone hookup stations, officially known as "public correspondence stations," are hundreds of feet high.

From a practical point of view, then, and maybe the government isn't so dumb after all, range from one boat to another is rather limited and interference thereby materially reduced; but range to Big Daddy on shore is very significantly increased because he has a high antenna.

If you opt for VHF radio, make a few inquiries in your region first. Be sure people can pick up the Coast Guard and that you will be doing your boating within reasonable range. On some of the more remote waters in America you either won't need VHF, or it will be useless.

As noted earlier, there are 39 channels on VHF, with some reserved for commercial purposes. Channels 6 and 16 are mandatory on all VHF transceivers; the first is the intership safety frequency; Channel 16 is the worldwide safety, calling, and distress channel.

Channels 12, 14, 20, 65, 66, 73, and 74 are for port operations, intership, and ship to coast, with Channel 12 and Channel 22 used by the Coast Guard for nonemergency communications. Channel 13 is a navigational channel used for bridge-to-bridge communications to reduce the risk of collisions in busy harbors. It may also be installed on some drawbridges.

Channel 68 is the "yack channel" for noncommercial ship-to-ship, and shore communications to a set in your yacht club, fishing camp, or marina. Uncle Sam won't let two neighboring shore facilities both have Channel 68 because of interference. If two fish camps or yacht clubs are within range of each other, one must take Channel 9, 69, 71, or 78. Channels 70 and 72 are also noncommercial intership, like 68, but are not as common on small boats. Public correspondence channels (so you can call your wife at home and tell her the fishing is lousy) run from 24 through 28 and 84 through 87.

A marine electronics dealer can help you if you desire a radio. Add it if you work big water in a small boat. Besides, you can ask a similarly equipped buddy how the fishing is where he dropped anchor, and you can call home—a great convenience. Questions of safety apart, a marine radio is a tremendous accessory.

## Other Types of Radio

If you range far offshore, VHF won't meet your needs. You should add a form of radio known as "single sideband." A lengthy description is not needed, since this is big-boat stuff and beyond the scope of this book. With single sideband, abbreviated "SSB," you can talk over thousands of miles. It'll cost you, too. Even low-cost SSB transceivers run to four-figure price tags, and by law you must have VHF first anyway.

You may also hear a lot of chatter about a form of radio known as Citizens Band, or CB for short. It is the cheapest form of two-way radio you can buy. It is also the least reliable. CB is so cheap you can pick up walkie-talkies in the discount stores for $10 or less. They need not be licensed, since their power is extremely low—by law, not over 100 milliwatts. That's one-tenth of a watt, if I put my decimal point in the right place.

A few random observations on CB are in order: When it first appeared, it was very good. It was intended for the citizen who needed radio for his business or personal life. You could install a set in your home, more in your car, office, truck or whatever, and have your own radio network.

Unfortunately, CB has been rendered all but worthless by the so-called "citizens." People buy linear amplifiers, which boost the output to illegal limits, then talk over great distances as if they were operating ham radios. Truckers, among others, have adopted CB, and happy calls now permeate the air: "Big Red, this is Fat Cat, toolin' down the Interstate, where you at, man?" These are illegal.

There are good, responsible people, like REACT, or Radio

Emergency Associated Citizens Teams, who put their CB to sound use; and you'll often find signs on the highways, "Monitor Channel 9" which advise campers and mobile home owners that CB users locally watch this channel to aid CBers who break down. Similarly, people with CB will pass on marine messages. *But the Coast Guard does not monitor CB and never will!*

With CB you have to depend on your neighbor, if you break down. Don't install CB until you have checked out the lake, fishing camps, and marinas. Never take CB if you can use VHF and have the Coast Guard within range. And be prepared to put up with static and plenty of interference if you use CB.

There is just one way CB can be very helpful indeed to the boat-owner. That's when you have a friend or another family that also owns a boat, and you make joint trips together. Pick up a pair of cheap CB walkie-talkies and put one on each boat, with a prearranged signal to turn them on at certain times.

Another disadvantage of CB is that they won't work when your boat is underway. Ignition interference will blot out any conversation. But they work fine when moored, docked, or drifting.

Due to the peculiarities of water, which materially extends the range, even cheap walkie-talkies can reach out to the horizon, or about five miles between small boats. For such purposes CB is a bargain. Private, two-boat intercom. Cheap, too. Nice if you have a cottage on a lake or bay. You can put a base station in the cottage and scatter other sets in car and boat. Otherwise, CB has too many disadvantages.

## *Man Overboard*

People fall overboard from boats. It happens all the time. This is why nonswimmers should be made to wear PFDs when out in a boat, especially children. PFDs keep them afloat until you can turn around and pick them up again.

The law requires you to keep a "throwable" PFD handy in the cockpit, in case someone does go for an unscheduled swim. If it should ever happen on a fairly large, unmaneuverable boat, the PFD should be tossed in the general direction of the person who fell overboard. The sooner the better. Even if the swimmer can't reach it, you have some sort of marker to guide you back to the general area where the person went overboard.

As any experienced lifesaver will tell you, never go into the water to save someone. Throw them an object, like a life ring, or a line. Don't let them get their panicky hands on you unless you are an expert.

On larger, less maneuverable boats, one person on board should be instantly appointed to keep an eye on the man or woman in the water, guiding the skipper back.

In highly maneuverable small boats you can (and should) turn instantly toward the side over which the swimmer fell, circle back, shift into neutral as you come up on the swimmer, and haul him over the side.

Kill the engine if they elect to come over the stern of outboard or sterndrive, stepping up on the cavitation plate of the engine. It's a handy and acceptable trick for reboarding such craft, but a no-no with the engine running. Knock it accidentally in gear and someone could lose a foot to the propeller.

Reboarding is easier and safer if you carry a ladder for the purpose, particularly if the boarder is no longer youthful, supple and agile.

## *Running Aground*

The skipper hasn't lived who never put a boat on a shoal. It's inevitable, like flat tires on an old auto.

The lovely part of owning a small boat is that when all else fails you can just jump overside and manhandle the hull into deeper water. This is true only of smaller boats.

If you have doubts about depths, and suspect shoals, go slowly. At slow speeds, you don't pile up so far onto a shoal. The minute you hit a shoal or bar, reverse the engine and boost the throttle up. It must be done instantly. This is because your wake follows you onto the shoal, and forms a little wave that tends to lift the hull slightly. Combine a reversed engine with the lift of this wake wave, and often you can back off within seconds of striking the shoal.

If that doesn't work, sometimes you can reduce draft by making all hands stand on the same side of the boat. Maybe then you can shove it off easily. Heeling the boat often works with deep vee hulls, but can be a dismal failure with a flat-bottom boat. Put an anchor on a buoyant cushion (or two cushions) and swim it out into the channel. Hauling on the line to the anchor, set in deeper water, while others also shove from the shoal, can cure even a stubborn case. Sometimes in coastal waters you have to wait for higher tides. Or you may get a line from a passing boat, which can help pull you off.

One trick worth remembering: If another boat can wallow by at mushing, sub-planing speed, pulling the highest possible wake, it can help you get off. I did exactly that with a 40-foot sailing yacht that was hard aground, and got it off by making a large wake. The wake wave freed the stuck yacht.

## *Towing or Being Towed*

Sooner or later you'll find yourself on one end or the other of a tow line.

Small boats tow best with a line to the towing eye, down on the stem of the boat—the one you hook your trailer winch cable to when hauling the boat. Keep this fact in mind. It's best for the towed boat to supply the line, at least with small powerboats. The tow-ee can have it made fast through the eye, or on a bow cleat, and pass the rest to the tow-er. And the tow-er, when he gets to launching ramp or finger pier, can cast off the towed boat and let it carry its way gently to the pier or ramp surface.

If you tow a larger boat—and it can happen, for I have towed boats over 40 feet long with little outboards down to 16 feet in length—you'll have to rig up like a Mississippi towboat, which actually pushes rather than pulls.

Lay your small boat alongside the larger one. Lash the two together with the docklines, but not tightly. A line from your bow, led aft to a cleat on or near the stern of the other boat, is the main "tow" line. A pair or so of breast lines keeps the boats together; your bow "after spring" line takes the strain. Rig plenty of fenders, pressing buoyant cushions into service if need be.

Obviously you aren't actually towing the larger boat. You'd find, if you tried it, that you can't. The bigger hull keeps pulling the smaller boat all over the place, and you may both wind up in the shoals or the bushes lining a channel. Tying alongside a large hull is often the only way you can take in a disabled big boat.

When you tow smaller boats, shift a little weight aft, and take the people off onto your boat. Don't let anyone ride in a small, towed boat if you can help it; and if they do, make them sit aft rather than forward, which would make the bows dig in.

*Check all cleats before towing anyone!* Cleats that are not through-bolted and backed may pull out under strain. The snapping of the stretched tow line can make the cleat a missile, and someone can be injured or killed. Do not trust weak, cheap cleats that are only screwed down. If you think the cleats are not up to the job, pass a line around the hull or cabin.

If you do your homework carefully and take care of your own boat, you will never be the tow-ee in such cases, some of which do have comic aspects. You will always be the tow-er, and it's a good feeling. People don't really like being towed in, find it embarrassing, and oddly enough they rarely thank you for the tow.

Take care of your boat, be able to meet emergencies yourself, and you'll never be towed in.

# BASIC NAVIGATION

Everybody's a navigator. Any time you tell your wife you'll pick her up at the beauty parlor at four o'clock you're navigating. You roughed out in your mind the distance, probable traffic, and average speed you could maintain, and came up with an estimated time of arrival, which mariners refer to as an "ETA."

Boaters need some form of navigation, even on rivers and small lakes. It may be nothing more than knowing the speed of your boat, and distances on the water, so you can tell someone you'll meet him off Rum Bottle Cove at four o'clock, or whatever.

On coastal waters there's a little more sophistication to it. Some of the fun in boating is venturing into strange waters, and they become home waters when you know how to use charts and a compass. Let's take a close look at the compass first.

## *The Mariner's Compass*

### *THE RIGHT ONE*

Unlike the Boy Scout compass you dabbled with as a youngster, a mariner's compass is more than just a magnetized needle perched on a pin bearing. The mariner's compass has a card rather than a needle (there are exceptions), with two magnets beneath it. The card carries the directions, cardinal and intercardinal usually being well-marked. As a rule, all directions are in degrees, with 000 at north, 090 for east, 180 south, 270 west and so on through a 360-degree circle. Mariners always use all three figures, and never speak of, say, steering "90 degrees." They steer a course of "zero nine zero degrees."

The magnetized card remains steady, its north in line with the earth's magnetic north, no matter how you turn the boat. There's a "lubber line" on the compass, which is aligned with the keel, or fore and aft line of the boat. As the boat swings around in a clockwise circle from north, the line appears first opposite northeast, then east, and so on. The card seems to move, but it is actually the boat.

To steer east, you turn the boat so the lubber line is on east. To steer a course of, say, 287 degrees, you steer to put that exact reading on the lubber line. Actually, small boat compasses are usually marked in increments of five or more degrees and you have to guess at it. But it gets you where you want to go, believe it or not.

All but the very cheapest marine compasses are "wet," meaning the card floats on a liquid. Most of the weight may be on a bearing that should be jeweled, but the liquid serves to damp the tendency of a compass card to oscillate in rough water. It may be alcohol and water, or a petroleum product. More viscous liquids damp motion even further, and are used only in expensive, "high-speed" compasses.

Most average compasses have adjustable secondary magnets in the base, which can be rotated. They help in compensating a compass for outside magnetic influences which produce an error known as "deviation." One magnet on a shaft will have a slotted screwdriver hole marked "N-S" and the other will be marked "E-W." They are used in compensating a compass, about which more in a moment. Cheap compasses cannot be adjusted. Some very costly ones lack these adjustments, too, and you must use deck magnets—a rather complex procedure out of place on small boats. So be sure you buy a wet compass, and that it can be adjusted.

A good buying trick is to quickly rotate a compass on the shelf or counter. Don't spin it; just turn it rapidly a quarter-turn or so. The card should remain steady. It should not try to follow the compass. If it does, you have poor bearings, no liquid, or a bad compass generally. Avoid any compass that shifts noticeably several degrees when you turn it, unless it all but snaps back in place. It should not drag, moving several degrees out of line and hanging there when you turn the compass in the store.

Buy the best type for your boat. Some are meant to be mounted

*A good flush-mount compass is ideal for larger boats.*

on bulkheads, some atop consoles, some are flush-mounts, and others are hung in gimbals, or brackets.

Flush mounts are better since they transmit less vibration than bracket-mount compasses, but they are tougher to install since a hole must be cut.

If anyone offers you a second-hand compass off another boat, it may be a bargain. See if it works, and doesn't "drag" when turned, make sure it has no obvious defects, chipped, broken brackets, signs of heavy wear or abuse. If it looks good and seems to behave well, and if it retails new for $40 or $60 and you can get it for a tenner, take a chance.

But you'll have to "zero" it first. Here's how you zero a compass, or remove all adjustments made to compensate it when in service.

1. Put the compass on a book, set on a table away from metallic masses. Stay away from the refrigerator and stove, and use the living or dining room. Align the compass with the book, as on a boat.

2. Rotate the book until the lubber line is directly on due north. If it were a boat, you'd be steering north.

3. Now lay a second book down and press it alongside the first so they touch evenly. Hold this book down firmly.

4. Carefully pull the first book—the one with the compass—away, and rotate it 180 degrees. Just turn it around. Slide it back in place against the second book.

What you did was use the books as outside references to rotate the compass precisely 180 degrees. Go around now to the opposite end of the book and read the heading. It should read due south, since you used the books to make a turn of exactly 180 degrees.

If it is not, the adjustments are out of whack. Take a nonmagnetic screwdriver or coin, and turn the N-S adjustment screw to remove *half the indicated error*. Never take out all of it. Just half. What you see is the sum of errors for both directions, north and south, so you only take out half of it.

Repeat the trick until you can swing the compass from north to south, using the book trick, and it reads right on every time. Then do it again, this time on east-west headings. You have zeroed the compass.

## *INSTALLING A COMPASS*

You can't just stick a compass any old place on a boat. There are two vital factors you must carefully bear in mind when making an installation.

First, no matter where you put it, the lubber line must be absolutely aligned with the fore and aft line of the boat. Otherwise you have a "skew" or slew error. The compass will be off by a few degrees, always in the same direction, all the way around. Whatever means you use, try to align the compass precisely. Error will show up in time, and you can ultimately take it out by rotating the compass just a hair.

Secondly, compasses are affected by masses of metal, just as your Boy Scout compass was pulled out of line when you placed a knife nearby. Single-wire electric wiring is worse; electronic equipment such as tachometers, radios, depth sounders, radio direction finders, and similar gadgetry should never be located near a compass. Tachs should be at least 18 inches away; big radios two or three times as far away. Of course, you can't help having some wiring around compasses, but if you take single-current wires and twist them around each other, you cancel out the magnetic fields that would be produced by the current and produce no deviation of the compass.

Whatever you do, don't mess around compasses with metallic tools, don't lay ferrous metal screwdrivers, hammers, and so forth near a compass, don't place old-type tin cans near them. You can induce a deviation that may remain after the object is spotted and removed. It may happen some day. It happens on the best of little ships. The famed Captain Bligh, he of "Mutiny on the Bounty" fame, once laid his pistols near a compass—to his sorrow, for it loused the compass up completely. So try to keep ferrous (iron or steel) objects well away from the compass location. Ditto electrical and electronic equipment, and single direct-current wires.

## *EASY COMPASS COMPENSATION*

Most texts, and even classes in boating, make a mystery out of what is called compensation, which is adjusting a compass for local magnetic influences that produce deviation. If you'll compensate a compass by the technique known as "running reciprocals," it's a fast and easy chore. Professionals do it this way.

All you do is borrow from the books, in this case the two books you put on a table. Remember how you used the side-by-side books to reverse a compass exactly and precisely 180 degrees? Do the same thing with your boat. You can't use books, of course, but you can use a gadget known as a "sun compass" or "shadow pelorus."

Several types are illustrated. One is homemade. Take a good look at it. There is just a square plywood base, a heavy, ruled, diagonal line, a hole in the middle, and a sharpened dowel force-fitted into the hole. With ordinary hand tools you can make one in a half hour, even if you sand off edges and corners to make it look shipshape and tidy.

The ruled line—you can make it with a soft, black pencil—is the secret, but otherwise the technique is like the books. Suppose you set

Left: *You can make a "sun compass" from plywood and dowel.* Right: *A homemade sun compass and a manufactured one, which can be taken apart for easy stowage. Note east is to the left of north on sun compass azimuth scale.*

up your homemade sun compass somewhere near the magnetic compass on your boat. The vertical shadow post in the center must be truly vertical, so you may have to shim a corner of the base. Rig a plumb bob from fishing line and sinker, and make sure the post is vertical, not leaning like the Tower of Pisa.

Pick a fairly calm day, set out in the boat, and steer due east *by magnetic compass.* Rotate the sun compass, keeping that shadow pin vertical, until the shadow of the sun cast by the post is directly on one side of that ruled diagonal line. Check to be sure the magnetic compass reads due east when the shadow is right on the line.

Now turn the boat around and head back where you came from. This is a "reciprocal" heading, or a precise reverse of any given compass heading. Do not refer to the magnetic compass. Use only the sun compass. Steer around and place the sun's shadow on the opposite side of that ruled line; on the other side of the upright center shadow post. Get it right on the center, targeting it on the line as precisely as you can. You just used the sun compass as a reference to make an exact 180-degree turn, or to run the reciprocal. And you know that west is the reciprocal of east. So now check your magnetic compass. *It should read due west.* If the compass does not read due west, the difference is the sum of deviations on the two headings. Again, take out *half of it*—never all of it—just half. And don't forget to use a nonferrous tool. Use the adjustment screw marked "E-W."

Run it again to be sure you have eliminated deviation on east-west headings. With a good installation, on a small boat, you should reduce deviation to zero. At worst it should only be a degree or two.

Do the whole thing all over again on north-south headings. Steer north by magnetic compass; adjust the sun compass to put the shadow on the line; turn the boat to get the shadow on the other side of the post, on the opposite end of the ruled line. Your compass should then read south. Take out half the difference, and repeat to double-check it. This time, of course, you use the "N-S" screw.

Just like the book technique, in a sense. You used an outside reference to make a precise 180-degree turn, to "run the reciprocal." The compass, if accurate, reflects that 180-degree turn. If it doesn't, you can spot the amount of error and turn it out with the proper adjustment screws.

Why start out with eastward runs? Well, an old tradition says you "swing ship with the sun," so let's humor the ghosts of ancient mariners. But there's another reason. On most small recreational powerboats, the engine will be aft of the compass. When you steer eastward, the magnetic influence of the metal in an engine is perpendicular to the compass magnets. It can therefore pull the magnets out of line more easily. But when you are steering north or south, that massive engine is now more in line with the magnets of the compass, and cannot exert quite as much pull. So deviation is more apt, in the average situation, to show up on east-west headings, and this is the place to start swinging ship.

Given a decent installation, and proper compensation, you should have a virtually deviation-free compass on a small powerboat.

Even if you never "navigate," a compass is handy to have on big water. Rain squalls can be blinding, obscuring the shore. Getting a "bearing" on the cove you came from means you can confidently steer a course for the dock, even when you can't see two boat lengths in any direction.

Compasses can be useful on rivers, in more remote stretches. With any decent map or chart, they help you orient yourself, identify the curves as you pass, and keep an idea of where you might be. A compass is a handy gadget to have, even if you don't use it every time you depart a dock.

## *Making a Deviation Table*

If after running reciprocals some deviation still remains, and if you expect to do a little bit of navigating now and then, you'll have to have a deviation table.

Forget it if you have only one or two degrees of discernible deviation on any single heading, and never run more than, say, 15 miles on any one compass course. One degree of compass error, over a run of 15 miles, means you would be only a quarter-mile to one side of your target—500 yards if you ran nautical miles. That's close enough to spot most targets, even channel markers. Keep the big-boat thinking out of your small-boat operation, and you'll enjoy it much more.

However, if you are in the tiny minority who feel actual need for a deviation table, it's easy enough to make up. Find two channel markers or two highly visible objects marked on charts, which can be lined up gun-sight style. Find their magnetic heading, the direction of this "range" as it is known. If two conspicuous objects are on a direct north-south line, for example, it's great. More on ranges later. Now let's explain how easy it is to make up a deviation table from a known range.

This time you have to have a manufactured sun compass. You can't use the homemade type, with the ruled line. You must have one with a dumb compass card (no magnets under it) marked in the complete azimuth scale of 360 degrees.

On a sun compass card, *east is to the left* of north, or counterclockwise; west is to the right, or clockwise. They are reversed, and you'll see why the minute you try to use one.

Suppose you have two conspicuous objects, like large channel markers on pilings, on a north-south line, and you determine their magnetic direction from the chart. Line up the two objects, like the front and rear sights of a gun, with the keel or fore and aft line, of your boat, and your boat's compass should read due north, or south, depending which side you are on.

So line up your boat. When it is in line, rotate your sun compass so the shadow falls on due north (or south, depending on boat direction). Then slowly swing the boat around in a circle. Forget the range. Look only at the two compasses. *Compare them every 10 or 15 degrees.*

Write down any disagreement. If the sun compass reads 090 and the magnetic compass reads 093, write them both down. Go all the way around the circle, in 10- or 15-degree increments. When you have finished, you have a deviation table and can type it and tape it down near the wheel.

You know, to use the case above, that if you want to steer 090 magnetic, accurately, you must steer the boat so the regular compass reads 093. You have corrected for the deviation. There are other ways to make up deviation tables, but I suggest a table of comparisons for small boats. It's easy to understand, especially if you work, say, every 10 degrees all around the circle. You can set any course, glance at the table, and see what minor adjustment must be made.

Your local marine store may have a double compass azimuth scale on paper, with inner and outer rings. You just ink a line between sun compass and magnetic compass readings, all the way around the circle, and refer to this handy table when correcting for deviation.

Most conventional tables read only in the actual differences, say two degrees or three degrees. And they are marked "E" or "W" to show how you apply them. If you want to make up that kind of table, take only the *differences* between sun compass and magnetic compass readings. Write them down in a table, listing the sun compass azimuths on the left, like 000, 010, 020, 030, and so on every 10 degrees. Write the deviations down as 0, 1 deg., 2 deg., and so on—and usually they'll change very slightly. Mark them E or W. How do you know which? With this jingle: "Compass least, error east; compass best, error west." If your magnetic compass reads higher than the sun compass, mark the error W. How you use all this comes later.

## *COMPASS ERRORS YOU MUST KNOW*

We've talked about deviation, caused by interferences on board. More important, but easier to deal with, is "variation." This is error caused by the fact that no magnetic compass points at the true, geographic north pole. The needles line themselves up with the magnetic north pole, which is near Bathurst Island in the Canadian Arctic. It is well to the west of the north pole, to those of us in the U.S.

Variation is usually taken care of on charts by printing a "magnetic" compass rose, oriented to magnetic north. You steer a magnetic course, and if you plot all courses and bearings from the magnetic rose, you'll get where you want to go. Professionals and yachtsmen plot everything in "true" directions, and always convert courses and bearings. But the small boater can take the sweat out of it by always using the magnetic compass rose on the chart. If you start crossing oceans, then learn it the right way; but in a small boat it doesn't hurt to ignore variation. Use the magnetic rose.

For the record, however, there's a formula to follow in converting a true course taken from the chart into one that you can steer. First you convert true to magnetic by correcting for variation; then you convert magnetic to "compass" by correcting for deviation. The jingle that helps you to remember how to make these corrections is, "East is least and west is best."

So if you have:

Desired true course, 123 degrees.

Variation (from chart), 2 degrees E.

Deviation (from table), 4 degrees W.

Then, if east is least, you subtract easterly variation, and have a magnetic course of 121 degrees. But the deviation is westerly, or "best" and you add it, so you actually steer 125 degrees by compass to make good a true course of 123 degrees. Important note: reverse these computations when going the other way, from compass to magnetic to true. Add east and subtract west, deviation and variation.

If you want to be a navigator, and plenty of people make it a fascinating armchair hobby, take up the subject in depth. All we want to do here is show you how to have a compass you can trust, and how to use it with little work.

## *STEERING A COURSE*

One thing they rarely teach small boat skippers is that compasses do bounce around a lot in bumpy water, even the good compasses. So learn this trick. If your card starts swinging and you can't seem to steady it down, slow down and come off plane. Let the boat settle. Get on the right course. Pick out a cloud ahead, or orient the boat to a shadow on radio antenna, windshield, or whatever. Then hit the throttle, get up and run. Recheck it every ten minutes or so.

Clouds and the sun do move. And a final item: When you use a sun compass, remember that the sun moves one degree every four minutes. If you take much longer than that, start over. You should also use the sun to check on the helmsman. Anytime you are supposed to be on a straight compass course, and the sun's shadow starts creeping across the cockpit, the guy at the wheel isn't watching what he's doing, and is falling off his course.

## *COMPASS CARE AND OTHER ITEMS*

Take care of your compass. Protect it from weather. Maybe you can buy, or your wife can sew for you, a cover made from Dacron or

*"Walk" a small boat around in shallow water to compensate a compass easily.*

other synthetic cloth, with a draw string. Spray a little de-moisturant on the adjustment screws from time to time, especially if your boating is done on the coast. They can freeze up from corrosion, if not taken care of now and again. Recheck the compass when you add accessories that might affect it. And check it now and again for the plain heck of it. They do go out.

The best way to check a compass quickly, given fairly calm water, is to settle down on an easterly heading, then make a buttonhook turn (mariners call such a precise turn intended to head you back the way you came from a "Williamson turn," and there's a way to make it, but buttonhook is a better expression for small boaters).

Head right down your own wake, down the center of it, as accurately as possible. If the compass doesn't read very close to due west, maybe it's time to dig out the sun compass and give the boat a good check.

One more tip: With a really small boat, sometimes it is easy to use the sun compass in shallow water with a sandy bottom, like near a beach while on a family picnic. With a little help, you can literally "walk" the boat around in the shallows while going through the sun compass-running reciprocals routine, only you don't even have to turn the engine on. Aim the boat east by compass, set the sun compass, swing it by the shadow, and if the magnetic compass doesn't read due west you know what to do. It's a lot faster.

Just try not to exceed four minutes per swing—the sun moves one degree every four minutes. And don't work too close to noon—the shadows are too short. You may benefit from setting up the sun compass on deck; sometimes it's hard to read under a windshield or in a cabin.

Once you have a good, well-compensated compass, put your faith in it. You'll be guided unerringly, by this magic, magnetic finger—even if your target is only a channel marker just barely out of sight down the bay.

# HOW TO USE CHARTS

## *Seagoing "Road Maps"*

It horrifies mariners to see such a comparison, but a chart is like a road map, with this important difference: A road map shows you where you can go in your auto; a chart shows you where you cannot go in a boat.

The most important function of a chart is to locate shoals, reefs, bars, sunken wrecks and obstructions, shallow areas, banks, and flats—all of them loosely defined as "navigational hazards." Secondarily, it does indicate clear channels, and locates the markers that identify them. Just as you can use a road map to take an auto tour into areas you have never been before, you can employ a chart to cruise aboard your boat into waters you've never seen before. As you cruise, you refer to the chart, note those areas you should avoid, and pick out the markers that lie ahead. By jumping from marker to

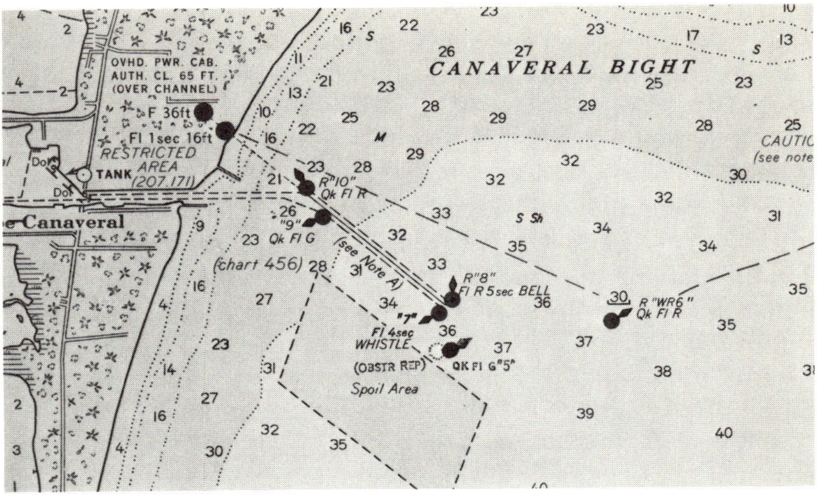


*Charts mark channels, aids to navigation.*

marker, passing each on the proper side, you can travel for literally thousands of miles without a problem.

Often the markers are within sight of each other. Sometimes they are not, and you have a short run by compass. If you installed it and compensated it as suggested earlier, you will have little trouble combining chart and compass to go almost anywhere. In today's fast, small powerboats, you would rarely be out of sight of a channel marker for more than a matter of minutes.

Coastal charts are produced by the National Ocean Survey. Millions are sold each year. They are available at many, but not all, marine dealers. Chart agents are restricted so the government can periodically check on them to be sure they come up to desirable standards. It is vitally important to have only up-to-date charts, and not obsolete editions. The government also sells coastal charts by mail. Write to the National Ocean Survey, Distribution Division C-44, Riverdale, Md. 20840. When you order charts by mail, send a check or money order for the right amount to the NOS, indicating the charts desired.

Ask for a free chart catalog. Number 1 covers the Atlantic and Gulf coasts, including Puerto Rico and the Virgin Islands. Number 2 covers the Pacific coast and islands, Number 3 is Alaska. The catalogs have outline maps of the coastal areas they cover, with the particular charts also outlined in color. There is a great deal more useful information on prices, and on other government publications, so that a chart catalog is worth having around for reference.

All charts are numbered, and as this is written the mariner's world is enduring the first stages of a conversion in the numbering system. Readers will be entering the boating world, if they had no previous experience, with the new system in effect, although some older charts will probably be around for years.

The new system, briefly, is worldwide in scope. All North American charts start out with the number 1, for the first region in the system. The continent is divided into subregions, starting with the southeast from about Charleston, S.C., around Florida to the Gulf of Mexico. So Florida charts begin with the number 11—or two ones. The subregions go counterclockwise, so most of the West Coast chart numbers would begin with 18, 1 for the region, 8 for the subregion.

Most charts we use will have five numbers, three in addition to the first two which identify the coastal area. As an example, the old Chart No. 848 covered an area south of Miami. It becomes No. 11465 under the new system. No. 847-SC described the waterway north of Miami to West Palm Beach; it is now No. 11467. The old No. 547, Miami Harbor, becomes No. 11468.

There's a uniformity that never existed before, and newcomers are fortunate in that they start out with the new numbering system and don't have to "unlearn" an older one. This makes it even more important to have a chart catalog on hand, since there will be some confusion for several years to come.

You may have caught the "SC" suffix on a number. That stands for "small craft" and is a special chart designed for smaller boats. It is a strip chart, accordion-folded, and encased in a light card cover. There is much information such as waterway facilities, marinas, ramps, and the like; tide tables for the area covered; hints on right-of-way situations, and more.

The SC charts mostly, but not exclusively, cover the Intracoastal

Waterway, usually referred to more briefly as the ICW, the Ditch, and sometimes less pleasant names. The ICW in two parts covers the East Coast from Virginia to Texas, although many people squeeze in a few extra Northern states and you can, in truth, run from Massachusetts to Texas on fairly protected water. It is the U.S. 1 of boating, and every inch is well charted and marked.

Charts come in several scales and "projections," but the differences aren't vital to the owner of a small powerboat. This essay covers only the basics. Suffice it to say that sailing charts represent offshore waters. Waterway and harbor charts are far more detailed and in a more favorable scale. Most charts a small boater would use are in the Mercator projection, which most of us learned in school.

Imagine a globe of the world in the center of a paper cylinder. A point of light in the center of the globe "projects" the map features out to the cylinder. That's the Mercator projection, and it obviously produces distortion as you move north or south from the equator.

But it is simple to use, and a rhumb line (the course line you plot) comes out as a straight line on a Mercator chart. The only thing you have to watch is that distances are different near the top (northern section) of a chart, and more about that in a moment.

When a tyro mariner opens up his first chart, he is usually startled at the wealth of detail. The most obvious information is water depths, which may be in either feet or fathoms. *Be sure you check the chart so you know which is which!* A fathom is six feet, and it's obvious that if you mistake feet for fathoms, you can run hard aground. Most inshore charts are in feet, so it should be no problem.

Water depths on Atlantic Coast charts are marked for the average of low tides, or mean low water. Pacific charts are mean *lower* low water, since one of the two daily low tides is markedly lower than the other. *Half of the month the water depths will be lower than shown on the charts,* and failure to know this puts even experienced boatmen aground. Obviously you should have some basic knowledge of the tides, although you don't have to be an expert with a planing boat that may only draw one or at most two feet when running.

You will also see tiny symbols for buoys, channel markers on pilings, and lights, and there are numerous abbreviations. Many are easy to understand: All floating, moored buoys have diamond sym-

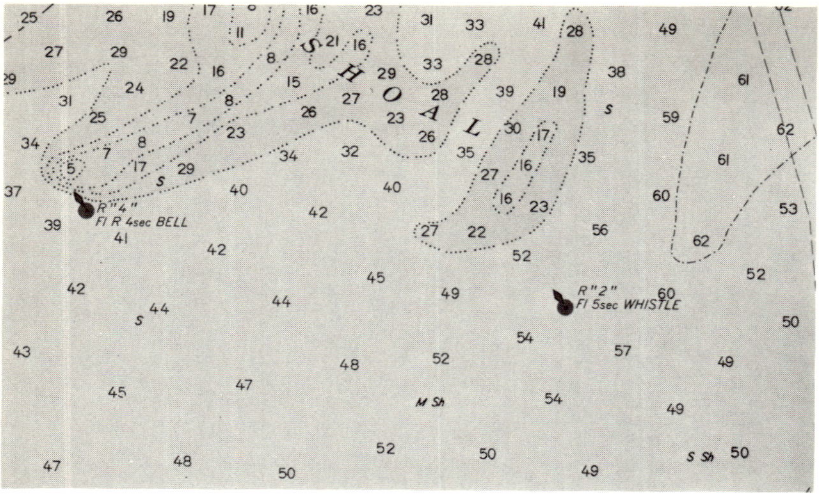


*Every aid to navigation is clearly shown on the chart, and no two in one area are alike, so you can always figure out where you are.*

bols, black for black buoys, red for red; and the buoy's actual position is *at the dot* under the diamond. Magenta circles around a dot mark lights on structures, and if there's a diamond symbol it's a lighted buoy.

A black diamond with magenta circle and dot may be marked, "'23' Fl 4 sec," which means it is a black buoy, number 23, with a white light flashing every four seconds.

A larger waterway light on pilings may be marked just with the magenta circle and dot, and the label will read perhaps, "E Int 6 sec 27 ft," meaning the light is white (because no color is indicated), flashes every six seconds with the light period equal to the dark period, and the light is 27 feet above mean low water.

One more sample: A magenta circle and dot marked "Qk Fl 16 ft '2'" means a quick flashing light, 16 feet high, and a channel marker carrying the number two.

Get the picture? Every "aid to navigation," the generic term for buoys, markers, and lights, is distinctive from all others in the area, and they are described on the charts in such detail that you know exactly where you are when you spot one.

There are other abbreviations and symbols, like "sft" meaning soft bottom, "hrd" for hard, and more. A whole book could be written about charts alone. The very best way to completely master all the abbreviations and symbols used on charts is to buy a copy of Chart No. 1. Order the free catalog from the National Ocean Survey, then order Chart No. 1.

It is not a chart. It's a booklet, in color, with all the symbols used on charts. The small boat owner doesn't need vast expertise, but it's a handy reference all the same. The price is not given because Uncle Sam keeps raising his rates regularly, but it was only 50 cents at the last printing of prices.

To repeat, however, the average intelligent skipper can understand the use of charts adequately enough if he just studies them with attentive care. They are not that complicated. And they fold a lot easier than a road map!

## *Piloting Information on Charts*

Anyone in a small boat can roughly orient a chart, opening it and holding it so the top (which on most charts is north) faces northward. Then you can pick out a target, like a buoy or marker, or whatever, roughly eyeball the chart and estimate that it lies south-southeast, steer that heading, and come up within sight of your destination.

But charts are so accurate that you can be far more precise in your "piloting." You can obtain accurate information from a chart on two major factors: distance and direction.

Distance may, on smaller waterway charts, be shown on a scale of miles, both nautical and statute, and maybe yards to boot. You can use the scale of miles on such charts. On larger charts you have only the latitude scale, which calls for an explanation: Latitude is marked in degrees, minutes, and tenths of a minute (there are 60 minutes to a degree). It is the scale on the sides of a chart, showing distance north of the equator.

Remember it as "ladder-tude" because it is like a ladder on the side of the chart.

On the Mercator charts, *one minute of latitude equals one nautical mile.*

To measure accurately the distance between, say, two channel markers well apart, you use dividers—available in most marine stores. Set the legs so they are on the two dots representing the markers, hold the setting, and transfer the dividers to the latitude scale. Put one leg on any convenient starting place, and let the other leg fall on the ladder. Read the distance as nautical miles and tenths. (As an aside, latitude scales on the general charts used far offshore for approaching the coast do not go down to tenths of a minute, but the average small boat chart does.)

What do you do when the distance is too far for the dividers to cover in one spread? Set the dividers on the latitude scale to any convenient distance, such as five miles. Go back to the first marker, set one leg down, then "walk" the dividers down the course line to the next marker, counting each step. Three steps would be 15 miles.

The final step will be less, so shorten the dividers to measure this last leg, go back to the latitude scale, and determine the exact distance you add to the 15. If it is 2.6, then your total distance is 17.6 miles.

With dividers, you can measure distances very accurately indeed, and if you also know your boat's cruising speed, you can come up with a running time and ETA.

Now for a word of warning: Always use that part of the latitude scale directly opposite the area where you are measuring distances. As noted earlier, there is distortion on Mercator charts, and the minutes of latitude vary in length as you go toward the top of the chart. Use your dividers and check; you'll find that a mile at the bottom of a chart is not the same length as a mile at the top. So work in the same general latitude all the time. If you measure a run in the middle of the chart, halfway between top and bottom, use the latitude scale in the middle, and so on. And a final warning: Never, never, never measure distances on the longitude scale, which runs across the top and bottom of most charts. It is not accurate.

Small boat skippers never use chart coordinates, but maybe

you'll read of a wreck or something, or a fellow fisherman might tip you on a good fishing hole, and you'll have to find it from the coordinates. Say it is Lat. 24 deg. 37.4 min. N., Long. 79 deg. 42.7 min. W. If it is in seconds rather than tenths of a minute, remember there are 60 seconds to a minute, or six to a tenth of a minute. Convert seconds to tenths of a minute.

Use your dividers. Work from the nearest parallels of latitude and meridians of longitude—the first are lines running east to west on the chart, the second are lines going up and down, or north to south. By measuring the distances from given bases on the latitude and longitude scales you can pin-point an exact position. You'll get the hang of it after trying it once or twice. It's worth knowing, even if you rarely use it.

## *Compass "Directions" on Charts*

"Direction" nautically speaking can mean one of two things. It is a course, if you steer it, a bearing if it is a sight or direction toward or from a charted object.

To plot courses or bearings, you use the "compass rose" printed on the chart—there are usually more than one. Use the one nearest your area. The rose is a circle marked in degrees, and oriented to geographic north. An inner rose is oriented to magnetic north. Use the inner rose to determine magnetic directions—the ones you steer or employ for bearings—and you can literally forget about the problem of compass variation, a phenomenon covered earlier.

There are several instruments designed to determine courses or bearings. Cheapest is usually the course protractor. It has a plastic base with an azimuth scale on it and a moveable arm.

Experienced mariners set it down on the chart with the center exactly over their point of departure, which we'll assume is a buoy or channel marker. They align the base with the nearest meridians of longitude and parallels of latitude, with north properly oriented. Scribed lines on the protractor base help. Then they just swing the arm until it touches the desired destination—another marker or buoy, for example. The compass course to steer is read where the arm intersects the protractor scale.

This method is fast and easy, *but it gives you true courses* and you must correct mathematically for variation—which is printed inside the compass rose.

The other way to use a protractor takes a bit more time, but eliminates the question of correcting for variation. Here's how you do it:

1. Set the protractor base down exactly atop your point of departure.

2. Swing the arm so it cuts directly through the center dot of the compass rose.

3. Now rotate the base of the protractor until it coincides exactly with the magnetic rose, the inner rose. The readings on the protractor base, and on the magnetic rose, as shown by the arm, must be identical.

You have now aligned the protractor with the magnetic rose. Now just swing the arm back, line it up with your desired destination, and read the magnetic course to steer to reach it.

If your compass is installed properly and compensated, has no deviation, or not enough to worry about, then that is the course you steer. It is that simple.

Most navigators will lightly rule a pencil line connecting points of departure and destination. They will label it, with the course *above* the line, distance *below* it, like so:

$$\frac{\text{C 073 M}}{\text{D 5.8}}$$

It means the course is 073 degrees (always use three digits, remember?) and it is "M" or magnetic. The distance is 5.8 miles.

You would mark the course with a terminal "T" if it were a true course, with a "C" if it were a compass course—the one on which correction has been made for both variation and deviation. Degree symbols are not required in this notation.

Some course protractors come with a bit of string instead of a plastic arm, and are more convenient on small boats. There are other types of plotting instruments, including parallel rulers, which are somewhat awkward on small craft. I have always used cheap, dime-store protractors I buy in the school-supply section. They're easily replaced if lost and work fine on small boats, once you get the hang of them.

Rule the course line first. Lay the cheap protractor down and line it up atop a parallel of latitude or meridian of longitude. Slide it along the line until it cuts the course line.

Read the degrees of difference where the course line intersects the outer scale. I say "difference" because it doesn't give you the exact course. What you see is an angular difference off due north-south or east-west, and it does take a little thinking to learn how to use it and convert the reading into a course. The only way to learn how is to rule a course line and play with the protractor until you see

*Courses and bearings are determined with the help of a protractor.*

how it works. And all courses are true, meaning you must make mathematical allowance for variation a matter of a few seconds once you memorize that jingle "east is least, west is best."

How you do it is up to you. Once again, we repeat that in most small boats you will usually just eyeball a chart and pick out a rough course by simple inspection—northeast, sou' sou' west, or whatever; and for short runs it suffices.

## *Other Charts, Other Publications*

All this pretty much covers coastal charts. Always keep them up to date. Never use obsolete charts. Edition dates are printed on them, and you can check with the dealer from time to time. Buy the new editions when they come out.

The NOS also offers other publications in addition to charts. Each year they print tide tables, which cost just a few dollars. You can determine the tides for any day of the year in advance. Current tables can be very useful if you live near inlets, because you can pick times of slack water. They help experienced anglers, too, for they can tell you when currents may be sweeping past a bank or off a vast shoal, meaning gamefish might be gathering to feed on the concentrated bait.

Few of the millions of boatowners in the U.S. know of the *Coast Pilots,* marvelously detailed books describing the near-offshore waters and the waterways. Coast Pilot No. 4, for example, covers the Intracoastal Waterway from Virginia to southern Florida. It is virtually a mile-by-mile guide down the ICW. Backed with the visual aid of charts, plus a compass, it takes you safely and easily on a thousand-mile voyage—which can be great fun, even in a small boat.

In this modern day and age of interstate highways, no trailerboat owner is more than a day or so from the ICW and a launching ramp. With charts, a Coast Pilot, and compass, he can enjoy a rare vacation treat available to few people. You can sleep aboard, camp on lonely beaches, sleep in waterside motels or marinas, and cover hundreds of miles in a week.

So much for the coast. What about other areas? Charts of the

Great Lakes and their connecting waterways, Lake Champlain, the New York State Barge Canal System, and the Minnesota-Ontario Border Lakes can be obtained from the Lake Survey Center. Address is 630 Federal Office Bldg., Detroit, Mich. 48226. They also will send you a free catalog. Charts of the Mississippi River and its tributaries come from the U.S. Army Engineers District, 906 Olive Street, St. Louis, Mo. 63101. Again, the catalogs are free.

Millions of boatmen use waters covered by one of the three agencies listed. The charts are easy to obtain. If you can't find what you need at a local marine dealer, write for the appropriate catalog.

# *AIDS TO NAVIGATION*

In the previous section covering the use of charts, you learned what the basic buoy symbols are. Now it's time to examine the real thing.

Aids to navigation, as they are called, are located on all navigable waters of the U.S., including the coasts, Great Lakes, plus the Mississippi River and tributaries. They are maintained by the U.S. Coast Guard. These seagoing signposts have guided mariners since the very first one was planted in the Delaware River in 1767, and sophistication came with the first lighted buoy in 1881, established outside New York Harbor.

The system may seem awesomely complex, but it is really very simple. Shape, color, and number of buoys or markers on pilings tell you exactly what you need to know. With the aid of a chart, as already mentioned, you always know precisely where you are.

## *Characteristics of Navigation Aids*

All buoys are colored, as are markers on pilings. Red aids are supposed to be kept on your starboard side when returning from sea, or running upstream. For a long time the mariner learns this part by

*Triangular daymark shows which side to pass.*

memorizing the simple phrase, "Red, right, returning." The three R's tell you to keep red buoys or markers on your right hand when returning from sea. (In the Intracoastal Waterway you are "returning" when heading south and west—running from Virginia toward Texas.) Obviously you keep them on your left when going downstream, or out to sea. Black buoys and markers are kept on your port, or left side when "returning."

All black aids carry odd numbers, all red aids have even numbers. The shape is also important, for in dim light when you can't distinguish color or number, you still have a guide. All can buoys are black, portside buoys. All red buoys are conical, and are called "nun" buoys.

In the case of markers on pilings or other structures, red aids carry a triangular "daymark" or sign bearing the appropriate color and number; black aids have a square daymark. All of them mark channels. Pass on the wrong side and you may run aground. Small boats can safely pass close to aids, and sometimes on the wrong side, but it is hazardous for larger craft. Buoys are held down by "sinkers" and can shift slightly out of position; planted markers on pilings have to be set back from the edge of the channel, or they could collapse from erosion of the channel by currents.

There are a few other buoys of special interest. Red-and-black banded buoys, with the colors horizontal, mark channel junctions, wrecks, or obstructions, and the topmost band indicates the preferred side on which to pass. White and black vertically striped buoys mark the middle of the channel. Pass either side. There are a few other special-purpose buoys such as those marking anchorage areas, but you rarely see them.

Buoys or planted markers may be lighted, and may make sound signals. Bell or gong or whistle buoys usually mark the entrance to a harbor and are at the seaward end. They are called "sea buoys." A black and white, vertically striped buoy, with a gong and a structure supporting a light, means the middle of a channel into a harbor.

Lights flash in a special sequence, noted on the chart next to the symbol of the buoy or marker. Most lighted aids flash at a rate not over 30 times per minute. Quick-flashing lights, not less than 60 flashes per minute, mark areas where special caution is required—sharp turns, channel constrictions, wrecks, or obstructions. Always check the chart when you see a quick-flashing light. Quick flashing lights may also be used on the front light of a range, about which more in a moment.

Interrupted quick-flashing lights—a series of flashes in bursts, with about five seconds between, are the same as red and black banded buoys, and mark channel junctions or obstructions which may be passed on either side. Lights flashing Morse Code "A," or a long and a short, about eight times per minute, are the same as black and white midchannel buoys.

Any aid to navigation may have a white light. But if the light is red, it is the same as a red aid to navigation or a red-and-black striped buoy with a red band at the top. If the light is green, it is the same as a black, portside buoy or marker, or a red-and-black striped buoy with the top band black. White lights have no significance other than the flashing characteristic.

Study of the illustration will help provide a basic understanding. It is really very simple. The lights make navigation simpler at night, and you won't find two buoys or markers in the same immediate area with identical flashing characteristics, so you won't be confused.

In rare circumstances you will encounter another type of navigational aid—ranges. Ranges are two structures of different heights. When one is directly over the other, it means you are "on the range" or on a safe course. Ranges can be lighted, as in the case of those lining the entrance to a harbor, and that's why as noted earlier the front range light may be quick-flashing. Quick flashing means caution, remember? And you have to be cautious when using ranges, because they are usually planted on shore. That's where you'll be if you don't check your chart so you know where to alter your course.

It would be very rare indeed for a small boat skipper to enter a strange harbor at night, from sea, but I can attest to the fact that a range does provide an excellent guide. By keeping the two range lights in line, rear range over front range, you know you are in the channel; and you will pass close to a buoy where, by consulting your chart, you know you must turn. You leave the range here, but by this time you are well within the harbor and it is heavily marked with buoys or other aids.

## *Special Navigation Aid Notes*

All navigational aids on the ICW have some portion of them painted yellow, a band on buoys and a border on daymarks. As this book went to press, the Coast Guard announced a change in the distinctive markings of Intracoastal Waterway navaids. The yellow border on markers would, in time, be phased out and replaced with a simple yellow stripe under the number. Also, black, portside, daymarks would be changed to green because of its higher visibility factor. Otherwise, things would remain the same. In areas where the ICW coincides for a short distance with another lateral system, as happens when you pass through a harbor, the regular aids have a dual-purpose color identity. It will be a yellow square or yellow triangle. If you are running in the ICW, forget the shape or color of the daymark or buoy! Be guided entirely by the yellow mark. Keep aids with a yellow square on your port side (if heading south and west in the ICW), yellow triangles to starboard.

The yellow square can be on a red marker, but be guided by the yellow only—and a square means portside passage, so keep it on your left. If you let yourself follow the regular meanings of the aids, you will wander off up a river, down to an inlet, or out of the ICW. Once past the common area, you will be back on regular ICW markers.

A final note: There is also a uniform state waterway marking system (USWMS) which you may see in some waters. It's very similar to the U.S. system, except that shape of the buoys has no meaning. You will still have red and black colors, but on well-defined channels they are usually in pairs and you pass between them.

If you see a black-topped white buoy alone, pass to the north or east of it. Pass south or west of a red-topped, white buoy. And last of all, a vertically striped red-and-white buoy means a hazard between it and the nearest shore. Never pass on the shoreward side.

There are other buoys, but not important to this essay. And we can skip the subject of offshore lights, since few small boat skippers would venture far offshore at night. Characteristics of seacoast lights are marked on charts, however, and if you ever want details you can buy a copy of the "Light List" for the appropriate region.

One word of warning, however. Many seacoast lights have a "red sector" covering a potentially hazardous area. If you fish after dark near a seacoast light, and see a red light, then check your chart and proceed with caution. It may well be safe for small boats of shallow draft, but it pays to be careful.

Summarizing the question of basic navigation so far, if you combine a good compass with up-to-date charts and a knowledge of aids to navigation, you can take your boat anywhere on the major coastal and inland waterways.

We skipped such subjects as taking bearings and plotting them, because 99 out of 100 small boat skippers don't ordinarily need them. If you want to learn more about navigation, which can be an absorbing hobby in itself, take a Power Squadron or Coast Guard Auxiliary course and go on to advanced studies with that as a base.

Meantime, it does pay to understand the elements of what is called "dead reckoning," and in any event it is useful to know exactly how fast your boat goes at any throttle setting. That's the next subject.

## HOW FAST IS YOUR BOAT?

The cheapest, simplest way of determining speed on the water is to use a marine speedometer. The type designed for outboards and small sterndrive boats costs under $20 and is easily installed.

A pickup tube goes on the transom, with an intake facing forward. Water pressure in the tube, which varies with speed, actuates a tiny coiled Bordon tube which in turn moves a needle across a dial. The effect is exactly like those party gimmicks that straighten out when you blow into them.

These Pitot tube speedometers are inexpensive, and are quite durable and reliable, although subject to temporary malfunctioning when the pickup tube is clogged by weeds. They are also surprisingly accurate, at least over part of their range, and those I have seen have a calibration screw on the back. You can run a measured distance, determine your true speed at cruising rpm, and set the speedometer so it is right on the money within this range. There are also high-priced speedometers using other principles, too costly to be practical on small powerboats. The better ones even have an odometer to record distance traveled.

Many boatmen use an rpm table to determine speed from the tachometer reading at any throttle setting. If you have a tach, it's the ideal way to go. In brief, you run a measured distance several times, each time at various rpm, and then make up a table of the computed speeds. It's simple in theory, a little more tedious in practice if you work at every 50 or 100 rpm from low planing speed to the top. You're on a measured mile (or whatever) all day long.

And you must, when clocking a boat, always make your runs in pairs, which doubles the work. You have to run each way on the course, at the same speed, compute your speeds from the times recorded, and *average the speeds to cancel out any effect of wind or current.* Always average the speeds, too, *never the times,* or you can introduce error.

Measured miles are marked on the charts of some major harbors, but they are scarce, so you ordinarily have to set up your own "trap" if you want to clock a boat. Luckily, there's a very easy way, developed by this writer for smaller powerboats.

## *Setting Up a "Trap"*

Find a section of clear, straight shoreline with no shoals, rocks, or other obstructions, no traffic problems.

Then, with the help of any friends who may like to have the benefit of a "trap" for clocking boat speed, measure off a reasonable distance on the shore. Make it as long as you comfortably can, but try for at least 500 feet.

You can use a long tape, if you have or can borrow one. You can use your anchor line, but measure it exactly so you know its true length when taut but not stretched. It's pretty easy if two or more people walk an anchor line out a few times, one person leap-frogging the other until they've covered four or five spans of a 100-foot rope.

Maybe you can measure the distance between two prominent objects, like trees or large rocks. You may have to set up a marker at one or both ends. Stakes don't stay; strangers pull them up, not knowing what they are. Spray paint in a daub will last, if it isn't defacing property or the scenery.

Suppose you have two trees, and you find that they are 757 feet apart. That's plenty good enough for the average small powerboat not capable of racing-boat speeds. Now for the tricky part: Convert this distance into an equivalent time, to simplify later computation of speeds. If you want to know your speeds in statute miles per hour, multiply 757 by the constant of .6818181 (or a rounded-off, shorter version of this constant).

Left: *Measure a distance along a shore to set up a "trap."*
Right: *Clock your boat over the distance, convert times to speeds. You need only three or four speeds.*

If you want to know your speed in nautical miles per hour, or "knots," then multiply the measured distance—in this example, 757 feet—by the constant of .5924853, or any rounded-off shorter version.

If you wonder where those numbers come from, divide the number of seconds in one hour (3600) by the number of feet in a statute mile (5280) and you get .6818181. At a speed of one statute mile per hour, this is the (fractional) time in seconds it will take your boat to move one foot. Simple. It becomes the base (as does the similar constant derived from the length of a nautical mile, which is 6076.1 feet) for a simplified method of clocking a boat's speed.

You can use .68 or .59 if you wish, but it's no sweat with larger figures if you have a pocket electronic calculator. And the point should be made that minor inaccuracies aren't really important. You can be a couple of feet off in your measurement, and it doesn't matter, and a few figures off in your computation of "equivalent time." It's all still close enough.

For the record, those constants apply to *any distance you measure.* We're using the example of 757 feet, which comes out at 516 (forget the decimals) when multiplied by .6818181. That's for speed in statute miles per hour. For speed in knots, 757 × .5924853 equals 448.5, or rounding off, 449.

What do these figures, 516 and 449 mean? They are, in effect, the distance "in seconds." It's a handy conversion. To determine speed, all you do is clock your boat on a run over the trap, and divide the seconds into those numbers. You get speed directly, with no other folderol or mish-mash of mathematics.

Suppose you make the run through the trap in exactly 20 seconds. Your speed in statute miles per hour is 25.8 mph (516 divided by 20) and in nautical miles per hour it is 22.45 knots.

Once you have measured and marked off a "trap," and converted it to an equivalent time in seconds by applying either of the constants, you have an easy figure to work with—and it is always good, until the trees fall down, the rocks vanish, or the paint wears away—whatever markers you used.

So measure and mark a trap, convert the distance into "seconds" and write the figure down. You can return to the trap anytime to recheck your speed.

And all the work was done in setting it up. All you have to do is run through the trap, time it, and divide the seconds into the standing figure, whatever it may be for your trap.

If you want it in formula form, it's:

$$\frac{D \times C}{T} = S$$

Where D is the distance in feet, C is the constant, T is time in seconds and S is speed. To repeat the constants, they are: Statute miles per hour: .6818181. Nautical miles per hour: .5924853. Or, with only slightly less accuracy, .68 and .59 respectively.

Once you have multiplied D × C, you have a permanent, "equivalent" distance expressed in time. Call it "E" and your formula, once you have recorded the value of E for future use, is:

$$\frac{E}{T} = S$$

Incidentally, if you must establish your own marks on the ends of the trap, you can measure it to a predetermined length with a convenient equivalent in time. Make it exactly 440 feet long, and you can use 300 seconds—run 440 feet in 9.4 seconds and your speed in statute miles per hour is 31.91 mph. Make it 506 feet, and you still use 300 seconds, but speed comes out in knots.

Always make paired runs, as noted earlier. Average the speeds made each way, to cancel out wind and current effect. Obviously, you should make each run in each direction at the same throttle setting or rpm.

## *Statute Miles or Nautical?*

The foregoing may have seemed confusing because we were using two types of miles—statute and nautical. What's the difference? Well, a statute mile is 5,280 feet in length. A nautical mile is 6,076.115 feet long.

The statute mile was created by statute—by ordinance or law, in other words—and it is the mile we use on land. The British established this distance in 1593 A.D., almost 400 years ago. But the nautical mile is related to the earth's own dimensions. There are 60 nautical miles to a degree of longitude *at the equator,* so a nautical mile equals one minute of longitude at the equator, or one minute of latitude on a conventional chart (see the section on charts). And a nautical mile comes out to 6,076.115 feet. If you often use charts, where distance is measured in nautical miles, you want to know speeds in "knots."

As a brief historical digression, sailors hundreds of years ago used to toss a log of wood, borrowed from the galley cookstove supply, over the stern of an old-time windjammer, with a line tied to it. The line was knotted at carefully measured intervals. Passage of the line over the stern was timed—at first by reciting a pat phrase, like you count seconds today by saying, "Mississippi one, Mississippi two," and so on. Later they used a sandglass. The number of knots that ran over the stern in a given time was the ship's speed in the nautical miles as measured in those days. So they came to be called "knots."

They have long since stopped using logs, but the word remains in the language. Since they "logged" the speed, the record of it became a "log" and the ship's book is still called that today. The expression came ashore long ago, and even the White House keeps "logs" of telephone calls.

Getting back to speeds, you must determine your boat speed in knots if you plan on using regular charts with distances measured in nautical miles. For most people, however, statute miles per hour suffices, and it always reads higher anyway. Powerboat racers always use statute miles per hour, though navigators and airmen use knots.

## *Making Up an RPM Table*

If you have a tachometer, and set up a trap for yourself, you can make up an rpm table very easily. The fast way is to buy some dime store graph paper and a drafting device called a "French curve." Both are sold in the same school-supply departments. The French curve allows you to draw evenly curved lines.

To make up a table, first write down your speeds across the bottom of the graph, at any convenient scale and increments you desire, say, from 20 mph to 40 mph in two-mile-per hour increments. Down the left side of the scale write in your tachometer scale, from the full speed rating of your engine at the top down to wherever you wish. Make it in increments of 50 rpm if you want that much accuracy. If you top out at 5000 rpm, put that at the top, and work downward on the graph evenly, with 4950, 4900, 4850, and so on. Usually on small boats every 100 or even 200 rpm is adequate.

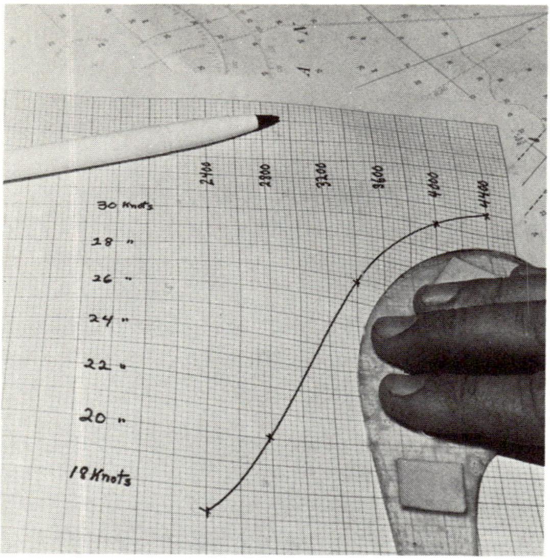


*Plot speeds and tach readings on graph paper, draw the curve, and you can pull speeds for any tach reading.*

*Labelmaker tabs can be glued down around tachometer for instant reading of speeds.*

With the graph, a stopwatch, and a trap, you can make up an rpm table. Make two runs on the trap at low speed, barely planing, at the same throttle setting and rpm on the tachometer. Average the computed speeds. Find the point on the graph paper where lines extended from the tach reading and the speed meet, and mark a tiny "x" at that spot. Repeat the whole thing at a cruising speed, about in the middle range. Mark the graph again. Make a final run to determine your true top speed, with wide open throttle, and mark the graph again.

Now use the French curve to link those three x's with a neat, tidy line, jiggling the plastic gadget around until the curve is fair. From this graph you can now pick off speeds at any rpm you read on the tach. You can type out a small table of speeds for various rpm, and tape it down near the helm.

But there's another trick worth using on small boats. It calls for a labelmaker, one of those gadgets that stamps letters and numbers on plastic tape with an adhesive backing.

Make up a set of speeds, cut the tapes so each one ends in an arrowlike point. Now stick those tapes down around the outside of your tachometer, each speed pointing at the corresponding tach reading. It's an instant speedometer. Glance at it any time while running, and you can have a good idea of your speed, whether in statute miles per hour or knots. No, it isn't quite as accurate as a carefully made rpm table, the preferred method of yachtsmen who are navigators. But it is plenty good enough for a small powerboat. And it is less work to make up than you may imagine, especially if you laid out your own trap near shore.

## *Speed, Time, and Distance*

Now you have learned how to measure distance on charts and how to determine the speed of your boat. From this you can plot a course (you learned that, too) and compute an ETA.

It's handy to know the formula navigators use, and you can memorize it as a "street address," "60 D St." That's all there is to it. Translated, it means that $60 \times D$ equals $S \times T$, or:

$$60 \times D = S \times T$$

Where D is distance, S is speed, and T is time—in minutes and tenths of a minute.

If you remember your algebra, whatever you take away from one side of a formula goes *under* the other side. To find out what time would be involved in running a known distance at a known speed, the formula would be:

$$\frac{60 \times D}{S} = T$$

And to determine speed from a known distance and time, it would be:

$$\frac{60 \times D}{T} = S$$

And to determine distance run from a known speed and time, it would be:

$$D = \frac{S \times T}{60}$$

Suppose you plot a course down a large bay, and the distance to the marker off the little cove you will visit is 11.7 nautical miles. You will cruise at 21.3 knots. How long will it take you?

Well, 60 × 11.7 = 702, and when you divide 702 by 21.3 you get 32.957 minutes, which is so close to 33 minutes that you forget the rest. That's how long you will be running, if you don't change your speed. Take your clock time, add the 33 minutes, and you have an ETA, or estimated time of arrival.

## *Dead Reckoning Simplified*

You don't have to be a mathematician to work out speed, time, and distance problems. Your marine dealer sells a little plastic computer wheel that takes all the work out of it. Many yachtsmen use them. I use a dime store plastic slide rule, much cheaper and more accurate. You can buy one and read the directions, on multiplying and division, and use the formulae above.

Some waterway charts also have a logarithmic speed scale printed on them. You use dividers. The charts that have the scales

*If you operate in "big water," you should know the elements of navigation.*

Left: *Dime-store slide rule makes math easy. Electronic pocket calculator is even faster and simpler.*
Right: *Materials for the navigator: charts, compass, protractor (or parallel rules), dividers.*

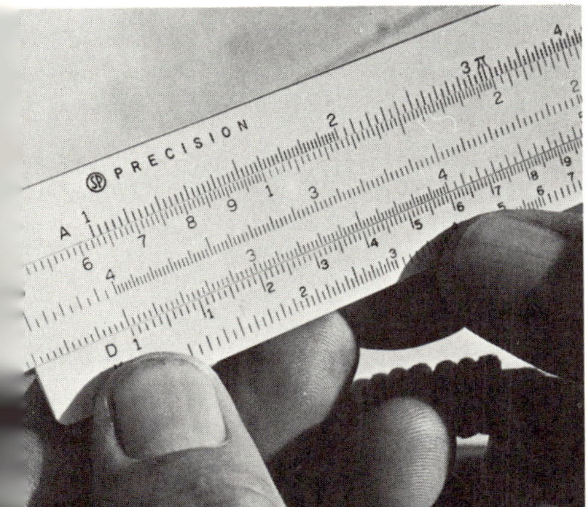

provide directions. What all this leads up to is this brief explanation of "dead reckoning," or navigation in its simplest form.

Historians ascribe two possible sources for the term: One is that it derived from "deduced" reckoning, since it was a deduction on your position. Another is that the ancient log was heaved over the stern, to determine speed, and sailors waited for it to float out from the "dead" water under the counter before starting their count of time.

Dead reckoning, regardless of how it originated, is nothing but the art of keeping track of all courses steered, all distances, all times, all speeds. You can do it graphically on a chart. Head out into open water on a specific compass course, run at a certain speed for a particular length of time. Convert time and speed into distance. Measure it off on the course line you draw on the chart, and mark the spot. That's your "estimated position," or "EP."

Even on open, empty water, miles from land, dead reckoning gives you a constant idea of your exact area—it is never precise, because of wind and current effects and obvious chances for human error, but you can always mark down an EP if you know how to correlate speed, time, distance, and direction.

The amazing thing about boating is that any skipper, with average instincts and sensitivity, ultimately starts keeping a subconscious "DR" in his head. You seem to always know approximately where you are, and can set a new course with considerable confidence toward a desired destination. It is described, in landsman's terms, as "having a good sense of direction" when it is really nothing more than educated instinct.

You won't do much navigating in a small powerboat, and may never need to keep a DR. But nothing gives you confidence like knowing the elementary steps involved. A good compass, up-to-date chart, knowledge of aids to navigation, course plotting, knowing how to relate speed and time and distance, lift you out of the tyro ranks in a hurry. Master these basics if you use your boat on any major waterway in the U.S., or even if you live within an easy drive of charted waters.

This knowledge adds immensely to the sheer joy of boating. With it, needless to say, you are a competent skipper and therefore a safe one.

# SEAMANSHIP SIMPLIFIED

Seamen have assembled, over the centuries, a sort of *lingua franca* of their own. Like pidgin, it is a conglomerate tongue, borrowing from many languages. Some words, such as "fathom," are Anglo-Saxon: The fathom, or six feet, came from a word meaning "the distance between a man's outstretched arms." "Beating" to windward originated with the Vikings, who invented the use of a pole called a "beitasse," and used it to stretch the edge of an old square sail forward so they could sail more toward the wind. "Frapping" is old French, and when a sailor fraps his halyards he ties them off so they won't slap and clang against a mast. The words "azimuth" and "admiral" come from Arabic. There are many more, so many words in fact that several encyclopedias have been assembled. Veteran seamen know many of them, because there is always a situation where only one word fits, and it's a sea-word.

Owners of small powerboats do not have to memorize a lot of strange new words, but they should know a few. Prime examples are "port," for the left side of any vessel; and "starboard" for the right. Starboard is old English, or Anglo-Saxon. The side of a ship was a "borde." Before the rudder came into use, old-time sailing ships were fitted with a steering oar lashed on the starboard side because most people are naturally right-handed. This side became the "steerborde," or steering side.

The other side, free of the encumbering oar, was the side laid against a quay for loading, or "lading." It became the "ladeborde" side. Ultimately the erosion of centuries made them "larboard" and "starboard." They sounded so much alike that orders were confused in gales and high seas, when misunderstood commands could result in vessels on the rocks. Only in the last century was larboard changed to "port," which retained some of the original intent. It was the side laid against the quay when in port, even though the rudder had long since been invented and it no longer mattered which side was docked. You may still find some salty old mariners on the Mississippi who say "la'board" rather than port.

Why the two words, instead of just left and right? Because on a ship—or small boat—you can't always tell someone to move to the right, or look to the left. He may instinctively go to *his* left when you meant the right. There are no planes of reference on a boat. So it pays to teach yourself to use the proper words. Port and starboard are unmistakable in meaning.

But there are other useful words: Say "deck" rather than "floor"; "bulkhead" instead of "wall"; "overhead" when you mean what landsmen call the "ceiling." (There is a ceiling on boats, but it isn't overhead; it's sort of inner skin of planking on wooden vessels. There are floors, too, but they are structural members.) Stairs, to a seaman, are "ladders"; and he goes "below" when going down into a cabin.

No owner of a small powerboat has to make a fetish of the language. Most people feel self-conscious when using it at first, anyway. But it does pay, in the end, to employ the right words and phrases when lubberly terms might be confusing.

One such area is directions relative to the boat. Anything in front is "ahead," and what's in back of you is "astern." (Although as a verb you do "back" a boat down.) Objects straight out to either side, perpendicular to the boat, are "on the beam," and you add port or starboard as a qualifier. Tell someone to watch out for another boat on the starboard beam, and he knows instantly where to look—straight out to the right-hand side, and it's the boat's own right, not his.

Objects at 45-degree angles forward are "on the starboard (or port) bow." Aft, they are on the "starboard (or port) quarter." These are parts of a relative bearing system that breaks down into the 32 points described in the section on navigation lights. It is falling into some disuse, and on most boats only the terms mentioned above are used, some of them slightly shortened. They are valuable, nonetheless, and a boating family should use them for convenience in communicating. It is rather sloppy and lubberly to shout, "Hey, looka there!" when you can be more precise. Directions relative to the boat are easily given in the described shorthand: Objects are on the (port or starboard) bow, beam, or quarter, or they are ahead or astern. That's eight relative bearings, and enough for most boatmen, who never really need the entire 32 points.

You'll pick up other terms, self-explanatory, on the waterfront. "Fore" and "aft," "amidships," are self-explanatory; closets are "lockers," and a clothes closet is a "hanging locker." Make it a point to learn the words and phrases you will need. There are only a handful. You'll find them useful, and you won't sound like a lubber around more experienced boatmen who use them all the time.

## *Learning the Ropes*

Old-timers weren't sailors until they "learned the ropes," which is just one of many mariner's terms that came ashore as slang. There were a lot of "ropes" on old-time sailing vessels, but when new rope was put into service it became a "line," not a rope, and carried the name of its function. There still are "ropes," but very few. Footropes, manropes, and bucket ropes are among them. But most ropes took a new name: anchor line, dock line, halyard (for hoisting sail), tow line, and hundreds more the small powerboat owner need not know.

Sailors also knew many, many knots and splices. There are hundreds of them useful aboard sailing ships and hundreds more that are obscure but do one job well. The old bo'suns knew them all.

Knot-tying knowledge is called "marlinespike seamanship," and it's a dying art even in today's fleet of sailing yachts. The small powerboat skipper can get by with a handful of knots, but should know them well. Fishermen worth their salt know such angler's knots as the blood knot, surgeon's knot, clinch knot, and more. They are superior to landsmen's knots.

Learn the basic knots, learn them well, and learn to tie them speedily—behind your back, if need be. You should also know one or two splices, hitches, and methods of coiling lines. Here's a list:

| | |
|---|---|
| Bowline | Clove Hitch |
| Cleat Hitch | Backsplice |
| Square Knot | Needle Whipping |
| Eyesplice | Flemish Coil |

All are useful on small powerboats, and are illustrated here in step-by-step photos, captioned so you can learn them properly. However, a few words of explanation on each may be appropriate. Let's take them in order:

1. *The Bowline:* They've been calling it the "king of knots" for many years, and it's true. No other single knot is so useful on any boat, regardless of size. A properly made bowline never jams, even when wet. It will not slip. Tied the sailor's fast way, it can be done in five seconds or less.

Maybe you learned it the "Girl Scout way." My wife did. She can still recite the method she memorized as a girl: "The rabbit came up out of the hole, went around the tree, and back down the hole again." That's because beginners make a small loop near the end of a line, grab the free end (sailors call it the running end), pass it up through the hole around behind the rope (sailor's call this fixed section the standing part) and back down the hole again. The rabbit makes a tiresome journey.

As the photos show, you start out as if you were making a common overhand knot (the first step taken in tying a package). But you "upset" the knot, turning your hand up and to the right. It forms the loop, with that damn rabbit already sticking his head out of the hole. And it takes one or two seconds. Then you pass the running end around behind the standing part, bring it back through the "hole," and set it up taut. Five seconds from start to finish. Try it, and time yourself.

Use the bowline when docking, if you have no eyesplice. Make a bowline, drop it over a piling, and cleat the opposite end on board.

*THE BOWLINE*
*A. Form a loop of the size required.*
*B. Start to tie a common overhand knot, but . . .*

*A.*

*B.*

C.

D.

*C. turn your hand up and to the right, carrying overhand with it.*

*D. This gives you a loop in the line with running part already passed through it. Steps A to D should take only about two seconds.*

E.

F.

*E. Pass the running end around behind the line, and bring it back through the "hole."*

*F. Completed bowline, made the sailor's fast, easy way. Practice until you can make a bowline in five seconds.*

With an extra turn through an anchor ring, it becomes an anchor bowline. Tugboat men link heavy hawsers with twin bowlines, their bights (loops) intertwined like chain links. It is the handiest knot you'll ever know, and you will use it more than any other.

2. *The Cleat Hitch:* An astonishing number of skippers who should know better grossly overdo the cleat hitch, wrapping turn after turn around the cleat. Actually, all you need to do is take one round turn around the base of the cleat, one figure eight turn around the two horns, and finish with a single half-hitch (which is nothing but a single, overhand knot, although it looks different).

*THE CLEAT HITCH*
*A. Take a single turn around the cleat base.*
*B. Make one cross loop around the horn of the cleat.*
*C. Finish with a half-hitch to hold it taut. You do not have to wrap and wrap and wrap the line around a cleat.*

*A.* *B.* *C.*

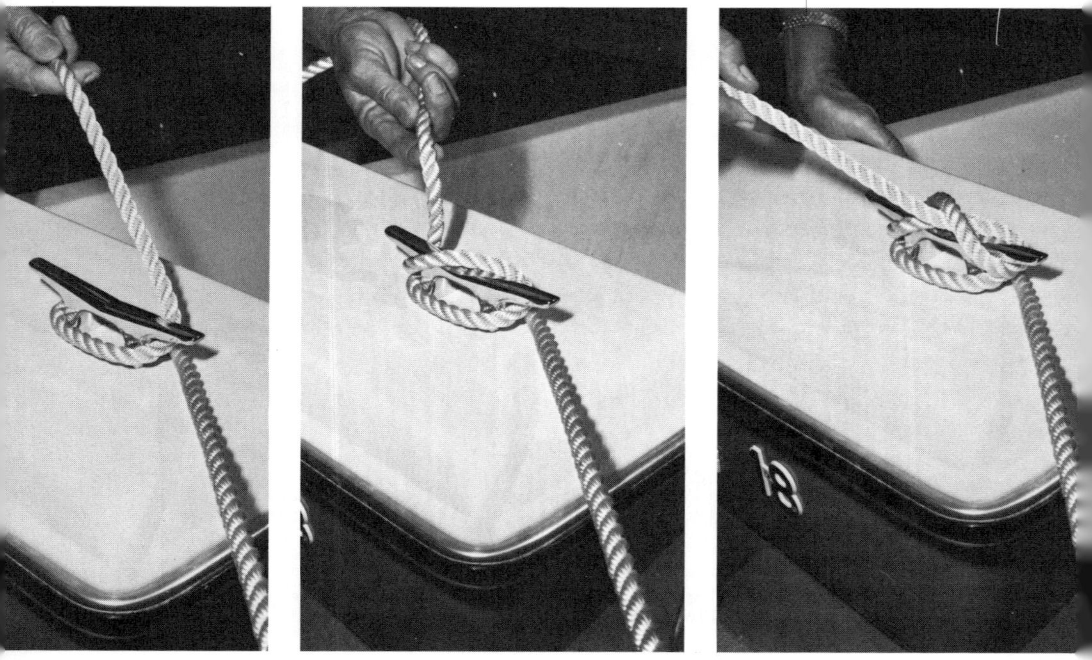

*THE SQUARE KNOT*
*The square knot is easily made. It's like two links in a chain, instead of the more confused granny knot most landsmen tie.*

3. *The Square Knot:* Landsmen tie a granny, which always jams. The photo shows how to make the square knot, also called the reef knot. It won't jam, although it can upset under heavy strain. Use it as a utility knot instead of the granny. To untie it, grab the end of one line and the standing part of the same line, one in each hand, and tug smartly. It will upset and come apart easily.

4. *The Eyesplice:* Follow the photos and learn how to make this very easy, most useful splice. With modern nylon lines, you will have

to tape the ends of the strands or they will unlay and leave you with a set of whiskers in your hands.

You make an eyesplice around a "thimble" to make up an anchor line. Make a tight, neat splice even if you have to do it over. The metal thimble absorbs all the abrasion from the anchor ring or chain, protecting the line from wear. Whipping the splice increases protection against chafe. It's the only way to make up a sound, secure anchor line.

You also make up ready-to-use docklines, of suitable lengths, with an eyesplice in one end. When you dock, drop the bight, or loop, over a piling, and cleat the other end aboard. If you'll be docking for a brief period—as at a fuel dock—reverse the line, provided you have open-base cleats. Shove the eye through the cleat base, double it back over the horns, and pull it taut. Then carry the line ashore and make fast with a clove hitch.

*THE EYESPLICE*

*A. Form a loop of the desired size. It would be larger than this for a dockline, much smaller if you were making it around a thimble for an anchor line. Note that the ends of the strands are tied (they can be taped). If splicing around a thimble, it would be convenient to tape or tie the splice to hold it on the thimble until completed.*

*B. Untwist the rope so you can pass the center strand under a strand on rope, as shown.*

*C. Pass the second strand (at left) under the strand in the standing part. Splice should look like this at this point.*

*A.*

*B.*

*C.*

D.

E.

F.

D. *Now you have one strand left, as shown.*

E. *Flop the splice over to the reverse side. It would look like this, with one free, untucked strand. It would seem it should be tucked from left to right, since that is how it lays. But . . .*

F. *Tuck it from right to left! Tuck it under the one remaining strand on the rope that has not yet been tucked. It will be obvious.*

G. *Pull this third tuck up taut, especially if splicing around a thimble.*

H. *Continue tucking strands alternately, over and under. It's wise to make three full tucks for each strand.*

I. *Taper the tucks with a knife. The easiest way is to cut one strand off, tuck the remaining two, then cut one of them short and make a final tuck in the last one to taper the splice neatly.*

G.

H.

I.

5. *The Clove Hitch:* Here's a very, very useful knot, commonly employed when tying up beside a pier for a brief period. The photos show you how to make two loops, inverting the second one over the first. Drop it over a piling and pull it up taut. For safety, since a clove hitch can work loose, most people drop an extra half-hitch on the line as shown.

6. *The Backsplice:* Not often used, yet very useful. Whipping, which prevents the end of a line from falling apart, sometimes isn't secure. A backsplice, while a bit bulky, completely prevents a line from unlaying, or coming apart. It's very easy indeed, and recommended for anchor lines especially.

*THE CLOVE HITCH*
*A. Pass the right hand under the left as shown to form a loop.*
*B. Drop the loop over a post or pile. Pull taut.*

*A.*

*B.*

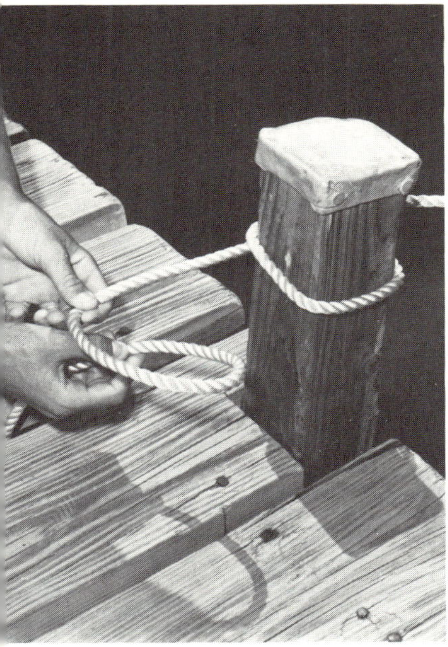

C.

D.

*C. Repeat the first step, right hand under, to form a second loop.*
*D. Drop the second loop over the first on the pile.*
*E. Pull up taut to form a complete clove hitch.*
*F. If docked for longer periods, add a "safety" half-hitch as shown, just a locking turn around the standing part. It will keep clove hitch from slipping free.*

E.

F.

A. B.

*THE BACKSPLICE*

*A. Unlay a bit of rope, tie the strand ends.*

*B. Form a "crown knot" by passing left strand behind center.*

*C. Go on by, passing the right strand behind the left end.*

*D. It should look like this at this stage. Complete by weaving the right strand in front of center one, then bring it from the rear back through that loop at left.*

C. D.

*E.*

*F.*

*E. Pulled up taut, the crown knot should look like this.*

*F. Now start "tucking" strands, as you did in the eyesplice, weaving them over and under the strands in the rope, back down from the knot.*

*G. Continue for three tucks, then taper as explained in the eyesplice.*

*H. All splices look better if rolled underfoot.*

*G.*

*H.*

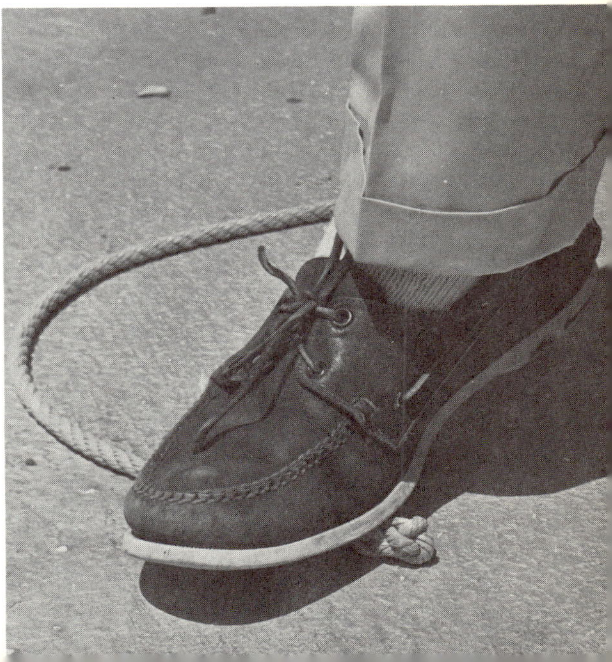

## NEEDLE WHIPPING A ROPE'S END

A. *Thread a large needle with heavy nylon thread. In the photos, waxed whipping thread and a sailmaker's needle were used. Tape the end of the rope so it won't unravel, thread the line through rope several inches from the tape. Leave a knot on end of the line so it won't pull through the rope.*

B. *Now wrap the rope* tightly *with thread, working toward the end.*

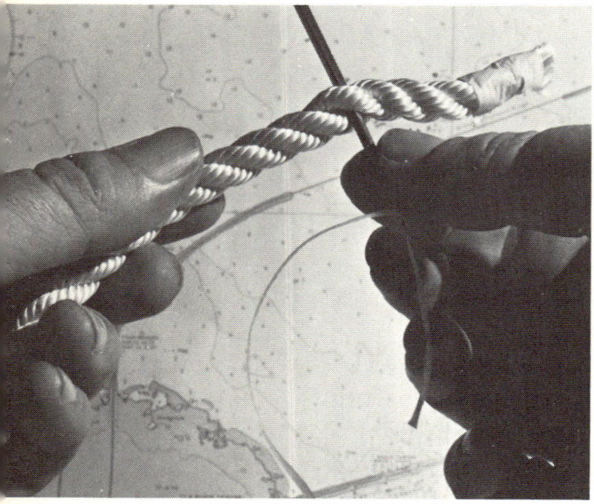

A.

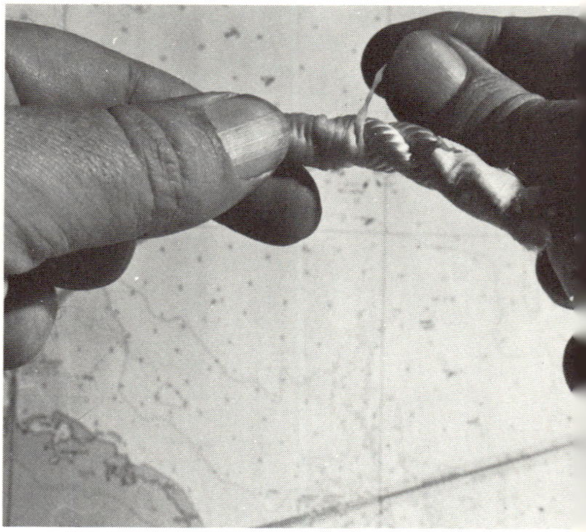

B.

C. *Pass the needle under one strand; pull the thread taut.*

D. *Lead the thread back down the rope, following the depression between the strands.*

C.

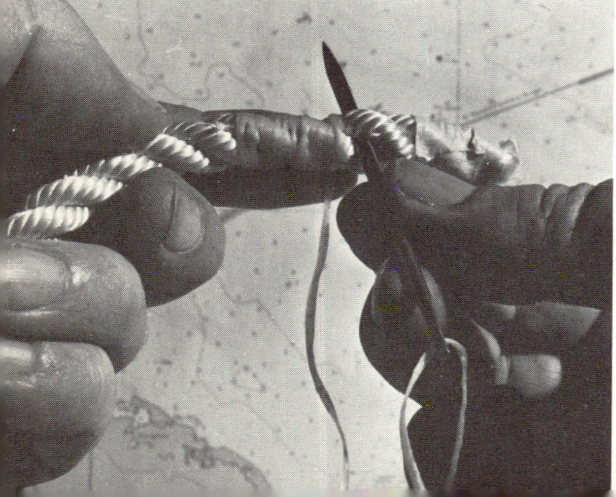

D.

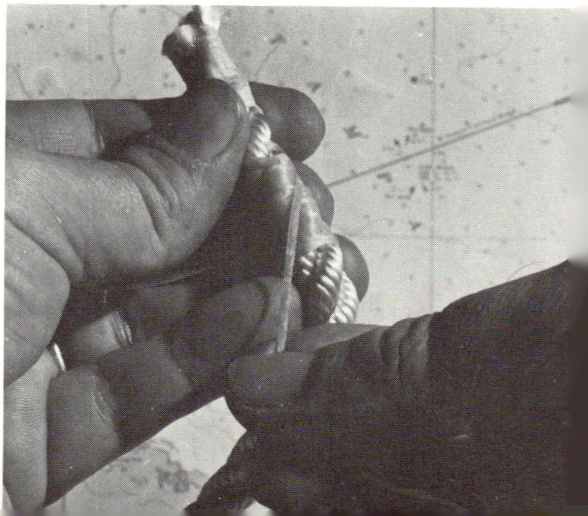

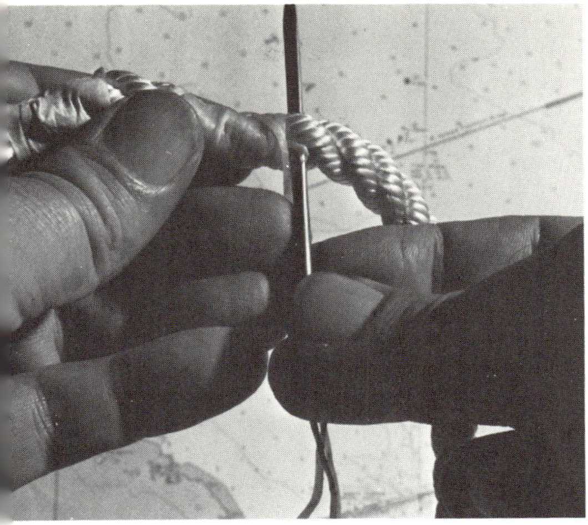

E.

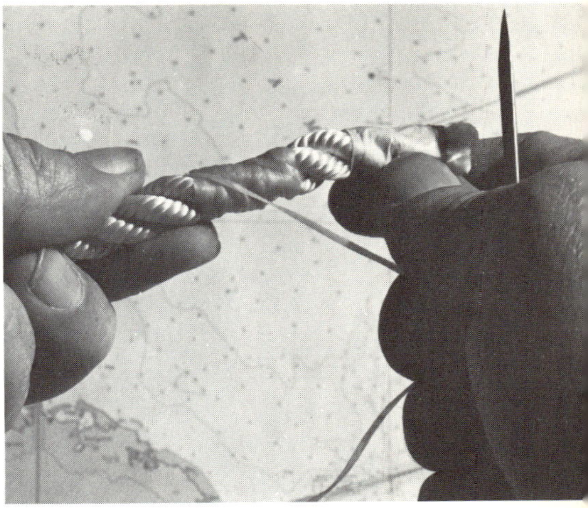

F.

*E. With the needle, pass the thread back through the rope, under the appropriate strand, in the opposite direction.*

*F. Pull taut, and lead the thread back down the next space between the strands toward end. Tuck again with the needle, and lead the thread back.*

*G. Make a final tuck with the needle. Pull the thread taut. You can finish with several turns around a strand, knotted, or by just threading the last of thread through the rope.*

*H. Trim the end, cutting away the tape. Completed needle splice should look like this. Takes only a minute or two longer than other whippings, is far more secure, and is the mark of a good seaman.*

G.

H.

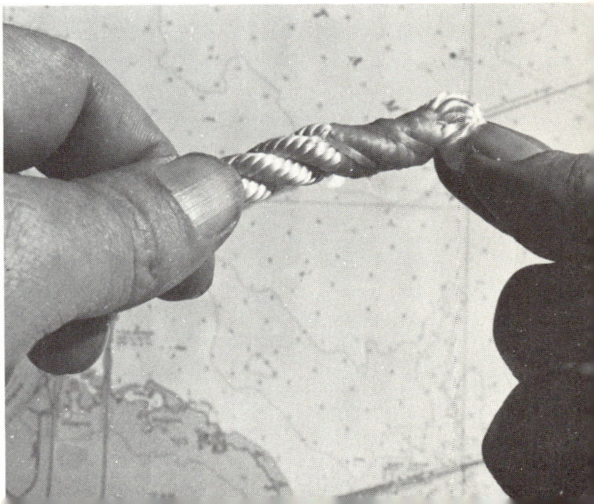

7. *The Needle Whipping:* Never, never tape the ends of lines to keep them from unraveling. It's the mark of a landlubber. Always "whip" them. Of all whippings, the needle whip is the best. It holds best, looks best, and again is the mark of a seaman. Few people can do it, yet it takes very little more time than any other, easier form.

The photos show how. You need waxed whipping thread and a sailmaker's needle, available in better marine supply stores. If need be, you can substitute nylon thread and a heavy-gauge needle of any type, but the marine variety is superior. Whip the ends of all line, unless you opt for the backsplice.

8. *Flemish Coil:* This is strictly a way to keep loose ends shipshape. You almost always have a little extra dockline aboard, after tying up and making your cleat hitch. Coil it down "with the sun," as sailors say, or clockwise. It snugs down idle ends and makes everything shipshape and "Bristol fashion." Flemish coils mark a good seaman and tidy skipper.

We've described a brief list of knots and other seamanship items for small powerboats. There are more. You can always find a good book on knots if you want to go further and make it a hobby. But do master those given here. They're vital to sound seamanship on a small boat.

*Coil all idle ends on deck or pier. This is the "Flemish coil" and marks a tidy seaman.*

## *Anchors and Anchoring*

Anchors have been around since prehistoric man tied a vine to a heavy rock. Today there are many types of anchors, and even a small boat skipper would find it wise to carry more than one. Here's a briefing on major designs:

1. *The "Old-fashioned" Anchor:* This is the one used as a symbol on cap patches and other nautical oddments. It is also called the "yachtsman's anchor," and the more recent term may be better since "old-fashioned" implies obsolescence and lack of worth.

Modern versions usually are designed so the stock folds down against the shank when not in use, making for easy stowage. Normally the stock is perpendicular to the flukes (blades) so it is bulky. When the anchor is dropped to the bottom and a strain is taken on the line, the anchor falls over on the stock, with one fluke now angled downward into the bottom; and with steady strain the fluke digs in.

Unfortunately the other arm and fluke is stuck up, and it can foul an anchor line if the boat swings with a tide or wind. With a reversed pull on a fouled anchor, it can even pull out of the bottom. But it is still a good holding anchor. This type, with narrow flukes, is called a "sand anchor," and as the name implies is very good in harder sand. It is in fact an excellent all-round anchor on virtually any type of bottom, but is bulky and awkward to handle and stow.

2. *The Navy Anchor:* Also called a "patent" anchor, this design came into use in the 19th century. It has huge, heavy flukes, and no stock. Weight was an important part of the holding factor. Navy anchors must be much heavier than a comparable yachtsman's anchor.

They were designed so they could be drawn up into the hawsehole, making for very easy stowage. Small navy anchors stow very easily on powerboats, too, even though you don't draw them up into a hawsehole—which you don't have, anyway. If heavy enough, they offer certain advantages. They'll grab quickly, even in mud covered with weedy growth, a combination that makes problems for other, more modern anchors.

3. *The Danforth Anchor:* This modern and highly efficient anchor was invented just before World War II, and won universal

Top: *This young boatsman is tossing a small "navy" anchor. He's holding anchor line in coil.*

Above: *Young boatswoman throws "Danforth" type of anchor.*

Right: *Woman boater hauls "plow" type of anchor.*

*"Fisherman" or "mushroom" anchor has a dish-shaped bottom. No anchor should really be thrown, as top photo shows. A tangled line can pull you overboard.*

approval after demonstrating its ability to haul landing craft back off beaches.

It is stockless, so it's easy to stow. It has very large flukes, designed to dig deeply into the bottom. In fact, the anchor often buries itself totally. Holding power is so good that it can be much lighter than yachtsman or navy anchors, is therefore easy to handle. It was invented by a man named Danforth, and it's still sold under that name, although many similar designs are also available. Some have an open shank with sliding ring, and are easier to break out of fouled situations where they are perhaps jammed. Reverse the pull and they literally slide out backward.

If there is an all-round anchor, it is this type, but they are light, and lack the weight to dig down through heavy carpets of soft, weedy growth covering the bottom. I've had them slide along for hundreds of yards during repeated efforts to anchor.

4. *The Northill Anchor:* This is a cross between the old-fashioned type, which is also known loosely as a kedge, and the more modern Danforth-type. It has the large flukes of the Danforth, but a transverse stock at the bottom, and it upsets to dig in like the old-fashioned anchor. Holding power is excellent, but unless it folds you can't stow it easily.

5. *The Plow Anchor:* Like the name suggests, it resembles a plow. Excellent holding power, awkward to stow on small boats.

6. *The Mushroom Anchor:* Also called a "Fisherman's Anchor" in smaller sizes. The big ones are used primarily for permanent moorings. Once buried, they have tremendous holding power. They must be weighty, however.

Fishermen's anchors are of dubious value except as so-called "lunch hooks" dropped for brief moorings in calm seas. Fishermen do like them for that very reason, however. They are easy to handle, but like the navy type they need a lot of weight.

7. *The Grapnel Anchor:* Like a fisherman's gang hook, it has a series of arms with rather small flukes or even none at all. Some old-timers call it a "grapple." It is useful for trying to fish objects off the bottom, such as a lost anchor line or an outboard engine dropped off the transom. It is an excellent anchor on rocky bottom, for it will hook under ledges quite handily. So handily, in fact, that it may jam in

place. Veterans who know the vagaries of this anchor will make their line fast to the crown, or bottom; lead the line up past and along the shank; and secure it to the ring with a light, breakable lashing. If the anchor fouls, a hard strain breaks the lashing and you can pull it out backward.

## *What Weight of Anchor?*

Experts have been trying for many years to come up with a universal table of anchor weights for various sizes of boats, usually on so many pounds of anchor per foot of boat. This writer has fallen prey to the same temptation, and has found this easy-to-remember formula that seems to agree with most of the others, while providing a little more flexibility for the various types.

Square your boat length. A 20-foot boat, squared, is 400, for example. Then use these figures:

Modern anchors of Danforth, Northill, or plow designs: two percent of the boat length, squared, for a working anchor. One percent for a light, lunch hook. Three percent for a storm anchor.

That means that for a 20-footer anchors ranging from four pounds to eight in a working size, and 12 pounds for a storm anchor.

Increase weight 50 percent for an old-fashioned anchor, and double it for a navy type. Don't worry about being exact. The formula is generous. You can sneak away with a pound or two less in working and storm sizes. Weight isn't all that important with grapnels. They depend on hooking under rocks to hold, and it's about all they're really good for. If you opt for a fisherman's anchor, get the heaviest one you can easily handle, and don't trust it in a blow.

The formula hints that everyone should carry three anchors. Many yachtsmen do. On small powerboats you can get by with two, but should never carry less.

Use the lightest possible anchor as a "lunch hook" for brief moorings in calm weather. It's a lot easier to use. For a brief period of time I carried a lunch hook so small it would fit in my hip pocket. It was a tiny, folding grapnel but with rather heavy arms for its size. It held a 23-foot boat in reasonably shallow water during good weather, and was child's play to work with. Never a single grunt or drop of sweat.

Carry a heavier one for overnight or extended mooring periods. Storm anchors aren't a must on small, speedy powerboats which may never be forced to anchor in heavy weather.

## *The Anchor "Rode"*

The combination of anchor line, chain, and hardware is called the "rode," although most everyone just says "anchor line" and lets it go at that.

We've already described how an anchor line should be made up with an eyesplice around a thimble at the end. It is very definitely a must, since it prevents abrasion and wear or at least minimizes it. Raveled line is dangerous. If it should part, you'll be set adrift, without an anchor.

So do make up a proper rode, with eyesplice around a thimble. Use nylon line. It has elasticity, which is valuable in service as an anchor line. You'll find that a three-eighths-inch diameter line is entirely adequate for boats up to 20 feet or so.

Connect the thimble to a short length of chain, using a screw shackle. If you worry about scratching the boat, you can buy vinyl-coated chain. Get about five or six feet for a small boat. The chain adds weight, but more importantly it decreases the angle of the strain, improving holding power. It also helps protect the line from abrasion on bottom. The vinyl-coated chain is a must for long-term economy, as well as added security and efficiency.

You can secure the chain to the anchor ring with an open link, hammered shut, which is more or less permanent. You can also use screw shackles. As an aside, the screw sometimes tends to freeze in place. I carry a rigger's knife (you're always looking for a knife on a boat) which has a small marlinespike or fid attached. It all folds up to fit in my pocket. If a screw shackle is stuck, I fish out the knife, open the spike, and pry the screw open—it has an eye in it to make it easy. Obviously even fisherman's pliers would work.

Make up a proper rode. It is cheaper in the long run. And you might find it convenient to carry two anchor lines. I have done so for years. One is quite long, over 100 feet, which means that when you anchor in a small boat there's a lot of line left over.

I also carried a line only 30 feet long, and use this when dropping the lunch hook in shallow water, not over five or six feet deep. I'd pay it out to the "bitter end" which is the end that is hitched on the "bitt" or old-time precursor of the more modern cleat. No spaghetti on deck.

Left: *A typical anchor "rode." The anchor is one of the modern and extremely efficient Danforth types, with short length of chain (vinyl covered to protect boat deck). The anchor line, with eyesplice around the thimble, is secured to the chain by a shackle.*
Right: *A screw shackle links it all together, anchor to chain, chain to line.*

*A good combination for average boat: a Danforth-type anchor with a short length of chain secured to the rope.*

## The Art of Mooring

When you decide to anchor, break out the ground tackle and get it ready for use. If anchoring by the bow, follow these steps:

1. Come up into the wind, slowly. Go into reverse to take the way off the boat.

2. Lower the anchor over the bow. *Do not throw it!* A coil of line could catch your ankle and pull you overboard. You can lightly toss a small and light anchor a short distance, but be wary. As a rule you should lower an anchor.

3. Either let the wind and/or current take you back, or go briefly into reverse to gather a little sternway. Test the anchor by holding the line in your hands. You can pretty much tell when it has dug in and is holding.

4. Cleat the anchor line, and if feasible, as when mooring overnight, snug down the idle end in a Flemish coil.

5. Take bearings on landmarks nearby, and check them a few times, to make sure your anchor is not dragging.

6. Enjoy your swim, lunch, dinner in a cozy cabin, or watching the sunset from the cockpit—whatever caused you to anchor in the first place. But do check the bearings from time to time to be sure the anchor continues to hold.

There's no law that says you must anchor by the bow. On most small boats there are often occasions when it is simply more convenient to anchor by the stern. It can also be easier. It's perfectly feasible in calm weather.

Just don't anchor by the stern beside a fairway, where large vessels can pass and their wake could sweep over your unprotected outboard transom. Ditto on offshore reefs where the wake from a distant freighter could similarly swamp you.

When it is time to raise anchor and get underway, use power to come up on the anchor until it is "up and down." Normally anyone can break it out by hand. Occasionally, if stuck or fouled, you may have to cleat the anchor line and go ahead on power to break it out. Sometimes, on lightweight anchors, you severely bend a fluke, but usually the anchor breaks loose. Watch out for the cleat; make sure it can take the strain.

## *"Scope" for Small Boats*

You'll hear talk about "scope," which is nothing but the ratio of anchor line out to the depth of water. The usually recommended figure is 7 : 1, meaning an anchor line of 70 feet for water depth of 10. In fair weather, on small and light powerboats, you can usually get by with far less. I've anchored on good ground with a scope as low as 3 : 1. With small powerboats, some of the "rules" for yachts don't apply with equal force. To define the problem with utmost simplicity, use enough line to keep the anchor from dragging. Often a scope of 5 : 1 will be ample.

A word on holding: In a pinch, you may need to boost holding power—especially if a blow comes up and you have no storm anchor. Securing your second, lighter anchor to the line some 10 or 20 feet from the first anchor already down adds extra weight, decreases the angle, and permits the anchor to hold better. It's a trick worth remembering. Occasionally, in some current conditions, you may want to

*Sometimes you can coil an anchor line on the bow deck, with the anchor in special chocks so it stays in place.*

*Deck pipes permit feeding an anchor line into a forepeak locker below.*

moor the boat so it won't swing at anchor. So put one anchor down off the bow, another off the stern. The boat will remain in place without swinging around.

Always "slosh" a small anchor up and down in the water to wash it clean of mud. Use your hands if need be to get hard lumps off. Never carry a dirty anchor below. That mud can leave permanent stains.

Stowage of anchors on small boats isn't easy. If you have a forepeak locker (right in the bow of the boat, below decks) you can install what is called a deck pipe. It has a cap, and there's an opening in the side. You can feed the anchor line below into the locker, haul out as much as you need when mooring. The anchor can stow on deck in chocks. Otherwise you have to find a place to keep anchor, chain, and line where they are readily accessible yet not underfoot.

Whatever you do, avoid these gimmicky winches, feeding line through a sheave at the bow, advertised to take all the work out of anchoring. Theoretically you crank the winch to hoist anchor, let it slip to pay out line. In actual practice they are awkward and unsatisfactory, besides being unseamanlike on small craft.

Anchoring is a bit of an art, but there's no great mystery to it. Follow a few simple rules, and you'll never have major problems.

# THE LAST "LOG" ENTRY

Writing this book has been hard work, but it has also been fun. The pleasure comes from the hope that one is being helpful. I would like to feel that many beginners, and even some small powerboat owners of some experience, will find the book useful. It was designed that way, anyway.

Boating can be an absorbing pastime. It can open the door to a whole new world, a world you'll taste the first time you walk a dew-covered deck in the early morning, when the water is like a mirror, reflecting the rosy bands streaking outward from the rising sun.

I would like to hope this book was the key to that wonderful door.

# *INDEX*